REGULATORY IMPACT ASSESSMENT

COLLECTION

CUADERNOS UNIVERSITARIOS
DE DERECHO ADMINISTRATIVO

[6]

REGULATORY IMPACT ASSESSMENT

Jean-Bernard Auby
Thomas Perroud
(Editors)

GLOBAL LAW PRESS
EDITORIAL DERECHO GLOBAL

INSTITUTO NACIONAL DE
ADMINISTRACIÓN PÚBLICA

Published by Global Law Press-Editorial Derecho Global,
and INAP (Instituto Nacional de Administración Pública)

In collaboration with The Center on Changes in Governance
and Public Law Sciences Po, École de Droit, Paris, France

Edited by Jean-Bernard Auby and Thomas Perroud

Editing by William Saindon Henley

ISBN (Global Law Press): 978-84-941426-1-1
ISBN (INAP): 978-84-7088-894-6
ISBN ELECTRÓNICO (INAP): 978-84-7088-896-0
NIPO: 635-13-024-8
NIPO ELECTRÓNICO: 635-13-025-3
DL: SE-2.318-2013

Layout and Design:
Los Papeles del Sitio

(Made in Spain)

CONTENTS

CHAPTER I
Introduction 11
JEAN-BERNARD AUBY & THOMAS PERROUD

CHAPTER II
Regulatory Impact Assessment: A Politico-Economic
Perspective 53
ANTHONY OGUS

"Regulatory Impact Assessment: A Politico-Economic Perspective": Some Comments on Professor Ogus' Paper From a Law
and Economics Point of View,
FRÉDÉRIC MARTY 73

CHAPTER III
Impact Assessment and Cost-Benefit Analysis: What Do
They Imply for Policymaking and Law Reform? 93
SUSAN ROSE-ACKERMAN

CHAPTER IV
Progress and Challenges in Selected OECD and EU
Countries in Developing and Using Regulatory Impact
Asessment (RIA) 125
EDWARD DONELAN

CHAPTER V
Assessing National Reforms Through Global Indicators.
Case Study 143
MARTINA CONTICELLI

CHAPTER VI
Outline of the French Practice of Regulatory Impact Assessment (RIA) System Preliminary to the Legislative
Process, One Year After the Enactment of the New 2008
Constitutional Framework 167
JEAN MAÏA

CHAPTER VII
Can You Teach an Old Public Law System New Tricks?
The Greek Experience on Good Regulation: From Par-
ody to Tragedy Without (yet) a *Deus Ex Machina* 181
GEORGE DELLIS

CHAPTER VIII
The Reviewability of Better Regulation. When *Ex Ante*
Evaluation Meets *Ex Post* Judicial Control 211
ALBERTO ALEMANNO

CHAPTER I

INTRODUCTION

BY JEAN-BERNARD AUBY
&
THOMAS PERROUD

CONTENTS

I. DEFINITION 14

II. THE RATIONALE FOR RIA 21

   1. The New Conception of the Public Interest Since
   The 1970s in the United States And France 22

   2. RIA and Quality 25

   3. Ria as a Product of American Administrative Law
   Principles 26

   4. RIA and the Better Regulation Program 29

III. THE HISTORICAL EVOLUTION OF RIA 31

   1. The Anglo-American Period: RIA as a Tool for De-
   regulation 31

   2. The New Turn: RIA in the Context of Better Regulation 36

   3. Spread and New Meanings: Models of IA 39

IV. CONDITIONS AND METHODS OF RIA 43

V. EFFECTS AND LIMITS OF RIA 47

REFERENCES 49

IN many Western States, administrative law is undergoing a profound change due to the pressures from the social sciences, especially economics, and from technical scientific disciplines, such as engineering and biology. In Europe, technocratic experts collaborate with the European Commission under its "better" (or "smarter") regulation initiative and with the OECD. These institutions are pushing Member States to evaluate policies using Regulatory Impact Assessment (RIA). RIA is a tool both to produce better laws and to reduce the costs imposed on business, citizens or local governments, particularly with respect to regulatory initiatives.[1] The EU/OECD initiative claims to espouse a coherent way of evaluating policies. The reality is more complex. Proponents of RIA urge systematic analysis using risk assessment and cost/benefit analysis, and they also support a heterogeneous basket of other goals, not all of which are consistent with the objective of balancing benefits and costs.

The move to incorporate RIA into statutory and regulatory drafting processes is linked to claims that legislators and government officials, when left to themselves, will produce statutes that do not concur with the public interest. In this respect, RIA is a new way of evaluating the public interest. IA requires lawmakers to balance benefits and costs and to seek the best overall outcome. Public input can help in the preparation of an IA, but it might also generate laws that more closely track the concerns of citizens, unmediated by representative or elite bodies. This is po-

_____

[1] Colin Kirkpatrick, David Parker (eds), Regulatory impact assessment: towards better regulation? Edward Elgar, 2007.

tentially in tension with the traditional concept of public interest as articulated by parliaments and judges.

Fundamentally, Impact Assessment signals an interest in the functional efficacy of the law. Under the IA model, the state evaluates statutes and regulations to determine the effects they will have on human behavior and on the achievement of public benefits. This much seems uncontroversial. IA counsels a focus not on the formal properties of the law but on how it operates in the real world. Precision, clearly worded drafts and consistency are valuable only as means to an end, not as ends in themselves.[2]

We will first try to define RIA (I), in order to examine afterwards the various rationales that underpin RIA (II). We will then try to give a historical account of the development of the tool (III), before moving to conditions and methods under which RIA is practiced (IV), and finally consider the possible effects and limits of RIA (V)

I. DEFINITION

Defining regulatory impact assessments is not an easy task. The purpose and content of the tool can vary greatly between countries. As a comparative report remarks: "like many things that are perceived as new, it happens frequently that different people use the term RIA with different meanings."[3] Further-

---

[2] This paragraph takes on the article written by Susan Rose-Ackerman, Thomas Perroud, Policymaking and Public Law in France: Public Participation, Agency Independence, and Impact Assessment, Columbia Journal of European Law, 2013, Forthcoming, Yale Law & Economics Research Paper No. 463.

[3] Italian, Irish and Dutch Presidencies of the Council of the European Union, A Comparative Analysis of Regulatory Impact Assessment in ten EU Countries, A Report Prepared for the EU Directors of Better Regulation Group Dublin, May 2004, p. 9.

more, much of the literature on the subject is concerned with what RIA should be and not about what it actually is. Both approaches are necessary to understand the phenomenon.

The most common misunderstanding is to equate RIA with the American cost-benefit analysis (CBA). As Susan Rose-Ackerman says, "IA is not quite the same thing as CBA, but it is grounded in an identical commitment to promulgating policies that have positive net benefits while at the same time improving public accountability and incorporating other values".[4] The misunderstanding is justified though as Executive Order 12291 uses the term "Regulatory Impact Analysis".[5] The difference between CBA and RIA could explain why RIA has not met with the same kind of criticism CBA encounters in the United States. CBA involves quantifying, in monetary terms, all benefits and costs of a project, be they injuries or human deaths. Some contend that quantifying human life is morally dangerous.[6] RIA has not suffered the same criticisms.

Both mechanisms will be studied here. Also, RIA should be differentiated from specific impact assessments (IA) tools, such as the one found in environmental law. These specific IAs pursue a different objective but share similarities with RIA. The aim of IAs is generally to evaluate the consequences of a project, both positive and negative.

---

[4] Susan Rose-Ackerman, Putting Cost-Benefit Analysis in its Place: Rethinking Regulatory Review, 65 U. Miami L. Rev. 335.

[5] The Executive Order 12291 establishes RIA in the United States for the first time. See http://www.archives.gov/federal-register/codification/executive-order/12291.html

[6] Robert Kuttner, Everything for sale, University of Chicago Press, 1999, p. 301. See also Amartya Sen, The Discipline of Cost-Benefit Analysis, 29 J. Legal Stud. 931 (2000); Henry S. Richardson, The Stupidity of the Cost-Benefit Standard, 29 J. Legal Stud., 971 (2000); Martha C. Nussbaum, The Costs of Tragedy: Some Moral Limits of Cost-Benefit Analysis, 29 J. Legal Stud., 1005 (2000).

The question is then: Is there a common concept of RIA that could be acceptable in most legal systems? If criteria differ, is there a core concept of RIA that would apply to all countries?

Pierre Issalys defines RIA using multiple criteria: it is a work of a scientific character, made by the administration in order to enlighten politicians, with results that can be made public. The purpose of RIA is:

1. to establish the likely impact of a policy proposal thanks to qualitative and quantitative data;
2. to assess clearly the problem to solve and the objectives to pursue;
3. to establish and compare the respective costs, advantages and disadvantages of the different policy proposals aimed at solving the problem previously identified (including the consideration of the do-nothing option); and
4. to conclude, on the basis of these elements with a justification of the policy proposal.[7]

For Radaelli, RIA:

"[I]s a systematic and mandatory appraisal of how proposed primary and/or secondary legislation will affect certain categories of stakeholders, economic sectors, and the environment. 'Systematic' means coherent and not episodic or random. 'Mandatory' means that it is not a voluntary activity. Essentially, RIA is a type of administrative procedure, often used in the pre-legislative scrutiny of legislation. Its sophistication and analytic breadth vary, depending on the

[7] See Pierre Issalys, L'analyse d'impact des lois et règlements : impératif d'efficacité ou condition de légitimité ?, in Interpretatio non cessat : Mélanges en l'honneur de Pierre-André Côté / Essays in Honour of Pierre-André Côté, Stéphane Beaulac, Mathieu Devinat (dir.), Éditions Yvon Blais; Pierre Issalys, Impact Assessment as a Means Towards Higher Quality of Legal Norms: Beware of Blind Spots!, in: Marta Tavares de Almeida (dir.), The Quality of Legislation, Baden-Baden, Nomos, 2011.

issues at stake and the resources available -the degree of sophistication should be proportional to the salience and expected effects of the regulation. Indeed, the expected effects analysed via RIA may cover administrative burdens or basic compliance costs, or more complex types of costs and benefits, including environmental benefits, distributional effects and the impact on trade. The scope of economic activities covered by RIA ranges from some types of firms to whole economic sectors, competitiveness and the overall economic impact of regulation. RIA can also be used to appraise the effects of proposed regulations on public administration (e.g., other departments, schools, hospitals, prisons, universities) and sub-national governments. Although RIA is often used to estimate the impact of proposed regulation, it can be used to examine the effects of regulations that are currently in force, for example with the aim of eliminating some burdensome features of existing regulations or to choose the most effective way to simplify regulation ".[8]

For Kirkpatrick and Parker, it is a "method of policy analysis, which is intended to assist policy-makers in the design, implementation and monitoring of improvements to regulatory systems, by providing a methodology for assessing the likely consequences of proposed regulations".[9]

The definitions are not always consistent or even completely satisfactory, but some common features appear. Firstly, the legal nature of the rules RIA is to examine is, to some extent, irrelevant. RIAs can serve to assess the impacts of any rule, be it a draft bill, an EU directive, a regulation, or an individual deci-

[8] Claudio M. Radaelli, Fabrizio de Francesco, Regulatory Impact Assessment, The Oxford Handbook of Regulation, 2010, pp. 279-301

[9] C. Kirkpatrick, D. Parker, Regulatory Impact Assessments: An Overview, in Regulatory Impact Assessment: Towards Better Regulation? C. Kirkpatrick, D. Parker (eds), Edward Elgar Publishing, 2007.

sion. Even though the proposed rules scrutinized through RIA may differ, they are usually norms of a general character, regulations as opposed to adjudications. Secondly, RIA refers mainly to an ex ante process. The purpose of RIA is to assess the likely impact of a policy. It can be used, though, on an ex post basis to review existing policies, but the process is different for RIA concerning future projects, as ex post RIA involve a process of evaluating existing impacts and not future consequences. Thirdly, RIA both refers to a procedure and a document containing at most a recommendation or at least some information on the positive and negative impacts of a draft rule. In this respect, it is a preparatory act whose content may vary from one country to another. It is clear though, that RIAs have no legal force, as they are mere recommendations to the authorities in charge of making the decisions. The purpose of RIA is to enlighten the decision-maker by producing a document to inform the decision-maker of the likely impacts of a project. Fourthly, it is a work of a scientific character, although the degree of scientificity may vary greatly from one country to another. In this respect, the competences necessary to carry out a RIA are various. The American form of RIA is cost-benefit analysis (CBA), and therefore requires strong technical skills both in economics and in sciences. As Cass Sunstein explains:

> "[A] government committed to CBA will attempt to analyse the consequences of regulation, on both the cost and benefit side. Such an analysis will include quantitative and qualitative accounts of expected effects, including, for example, a statement of the expected lives saved, curable cancers prevented, asthma attacks averted, and much more (…). Where science does not permit predictions, governments should produce ranges, as for example, in a statement that the regulation will save between 100 and 240 lives per year (…). Whenever possible, expected benefits should be translated into monetary

equivalents, not because a life is really worth, say, $6 million, but to permit sensible comparisons and priorities."[10]

In other words, CBA requires strong forensic skills in order to estimate the likely impact of a policy proposal and translate the estimate into monetary value. It can also require legal competences in countries where RIA is not limited to CBA, in order to assess the legal problems involved in the implementation of a proposed norm. For example, in France the law requires RIAs to explain the various implementation measures the proposed rule would require. Thus, the impacts taken into account in a RIA are manifold; they can be economic, legal, environmental or social. They can concern businesses in general or specifically small businesses, local governments, or central States. The projected costs can also vary from administrative burdens to concepts such as compliance costs or distributional effects. This explains why RIA production must be decentralized. One agency cannot master all the skills needed to perform a RIA and the sponsoring agencies or departments that are in charge of the final decision are also in charge of the RIA. Fifthly, RIA can be defined by its method. The method is to assess, quantitatively and/or qualitatively, as Pierre Issalys states,[11] the likely consequences of the different solutions intended to address the issue in question. The comparison of the costs, advantages and disadvantages of the measures should help choosing the best policy tool, namely, the one that minimizes costs while, at the same, maximises results. The method of RIA comprises several steps:
  • "The definition of the problem (in terms of risk, needs, opportunities for improvement on the status quo);

---

[10] Cass Sunstein, The cost-benefit state: the future of regulatory protection, Chicago, IL : Section of Administrative Law and Regulatory Practice, American Bar Association, 2002, p. 20.

[11] See Pierre Issalys, L'analyse d'impact des lois et règlements : impératif d'efficacité ou condition de légitimité.

- An approach to governance based on a transparent, accountable process of formulation of rules, with special emphasis on consultation, the use of empirical evidence in the preparation of legislation, and standards for the validation of natural and social sciences in the regulatory process.
- The explicit consideration of multiple options, including the zero option of not intervening, market-friendly alternatives to regulation, soft law, voluntary agreements, and traditional 'command and control' regulation.
- Specific methodologies for the analysis of different regulatory options, such as cost–benefit analysis, multi-criteria analysis, and comparative risk assessment.
- A commitment to ex-post monitoring and review of regulations."[12]

The purpose of RIA is therefore to inform the decision-making process by following these steps. As Adler and Posner put it, it is indeed "a decision procedure",[13] a procedure that aims to produce or favour certain kinds of decisions. In the US context, the goal of RIA/CBA is to produce decisions "whose benefits exceed their costs".[14] In other contexts, the purpose of RIA can be different according to national preferences, though it is possible to say that RIA concerns basing public policy on "neutral" assessments, on objective evidence. The comparative study of RIA in several jurisdictions shows some major differences and concepts

---

[12] See Claudio M. Radaelli (2005): Diffusion without convergence: how political context shapes the adoption of regulatory impact assessment, Journal of European Public Policy, 12:5, 924-943.

[13] Matthew D. Adler, Eric A. Posner, Rethinking Cost Benefit Analysis 109 Yale L.J. 165.

[14] Robert H. Frank, Why is Cost-Benefit Analysis so Controversial?, in Cost-benefit analysis : legal, economic, and philosophical perspectives, Matthew D. Alder, Eric A. Posner (ed), Chicago, University of Chicago Press, 2001, p. 77; Matthew D. Adler, Eric A. Posner, Rethinking Cost Benefit Analysis 109 Yale L.J. 165.

between the Anglo-American approach, which could also be termed an economic approach based on CBA, and a more legalistic one. This difference reflects the different concerns which the same tool (the RIAs) is designed to address.[15]

II. THE RATIONALE FOR RIA

Looking into the reasons that give rise to the birth and rise of RIA in Western states requires going beyond the traditional discussion of RIA and CBA. The traditional account maintains that only neoliberalism can explain the use of such a tool. This premise is valid to a certain extent.[16] The United States and the United Kingdom under Reagan and Thatcher promoted, developed and advocated the use of RIA, following a neoliberal doctrine that put business first.

We would like to show that this is not the only reason for RIA's development. Firstly, RIA could not have appeared if certain intellectual revolutions had not altered the concepts of state action and public interest (1). Secondly, an explanation of the development of RIA in the United States can also be found in the implementation of the Administrative Procedure Act, which has been termed the "adversarial legalism" model of policy-making (2).

---

[15] See Claudio M. Radaelli (2005): Diffusion without convergence: how political context shapes the adoption of regulatory impact assessment, Journal of European Public Policy, 12:5, 924-943.

[16] We will study this discourse in part III.

1. THE NEW CONCEPTION OF THE PUBLIC INTEREST SINCE THE 1970S IN THE UNITED STATES AND FRANCE

In many Western states, administrative law has undergone a profound change due to the pressures from social science, especially economics, and technical scientific disciplines, such as engineering and biology. The move to incorporate IA into statutory and regulatory drafting processes is linked to claims that legislators and government officials, when left to themselves, will produce statutes that do not concur with public interest. In this respect, IA is an innovative means to evaluating the public interest. IA requires lawmakers to balance benefits and costs and to seek the best overall outcome. Public input can help in the preparation of an IA, but it might also generate laws that more closely track the concerns of citizens, unmediated by representative or elite bodies. This is potentially in tension with the traditional concept of public interest as articulated by parliaments and judges.[17]

Fundamentally, Impact Assessment signals an interest in the functional efficacy of the law. Under the IA model, the state evaluates statutes and regulations to determine the effects they will have on human behaviour and on the achievement of public benefits. This much seems uncontroversial. IA counsels a focus not on the formal properties of the law but on how it operates in the real world. Precision, clearly worded drafts and consistency are valuable only as means to an end, not as ends in themselves.

RIA exemplifies this changing conception of the public interest. First, RIA shows that the public interests no longer stems from the will of the administration but from a balance of costs

---

[17] This part takes on the article written by Susan Rose-Ackerman, Thomas Perroud, Policymaking and Public Law in France: Public Participation, Agency Independence, and Impact Assessment, Columbia Journal of European Law, 2013, Forthcoming, Yale Law & Economics Research Paper No. 463.

and benefits. The public interest is no longer something the administration can declare unilaterally; it must be justified, constructed.

We find one example of such a development in the jurisprudence of the French *Conseil d'Etat*. This development is even more interesting as it intertwines the new concept of public interest with the idea of costs and benefits, and a necessary balance between both. It is also contemporaneous with the creation of impact assessments in environmental law in the United States and in France.[18]

French public lawyers have made use of balancing since the iconic *Conseil d'État* case of *Ville Nouvelle-Est*.[19] That case, decided long before the current push for IA, concerned the official approval of an urban development project and it dealt with the law of eminent domain.[20] The judgment mentioned the need for the court to make tradeoffs, or to balance (*bilan*) competing values. The *Conseil d'État* held that: "A project may not lawfully be declared in the public interest unless the infringements against private property, the financial costs, and the possible social costs are

---

[18] IA arose in American debates over environmental policy and later affected policymaking in Europe. In the US these debates led to passage of the National Environmental Policy Act (NEPA) in 1970 that requires an Environmental Impact Assessment (EIA) for all public projects that might affect the natural environment (National Environmental Policy Act, P.L. 91-190 (1970). For a history of NEPA and the introduction of the environmental impact assessment Rabel J. Burdge (1991): A Brief History and Major Trends in the Field of Impact Assessment, Impact Assessment, 9:4, 93-104). In France as well, IA developped first in the field of environment with a 1976 Act. Michel Prieur argues that this device is a « revolutionnary administrative procedure » (Loi du 10 juillet 1976 relative à la protection de la nature; see M. Prieur, Droit de l'environnement, Dalloz, 2011, at p. 91).

[19] Guy Braibant 27 AJDA 404 (1971) (reproducing his conclusions on the case).

[20] In France with its dual court system, takings case are rather complex. The administrative courts, as in *Ville Nouvelle-Est*, decide on the legality of the project. If the project is legally acceptable, disputes over the level of compensation are heard in the civil courts.

not excessive compared with the public benefits of the project." [authors' translation][21]

Guy Braibant, the *Commissaire du gouvernement* in this case, justified this evolution in the jurisprudence by saying that the *Conseil d'État* now has to acknowledge that the public interest is plural. He wrote that:

"There is no longer, on one side, the public power and the general interest, and, on the other, private property. More and more frequently multiple public interests are present behind the expropriating authorities and the expropriated, and it may well sometimes happen that the private interests that benefit from the operations will weigh more in the decision making process than the public interests the operation may harm. Thus, it is not possible to keep to the old reasoning that amounted to asking if the takings, in themselves, were in the public interest. The various advantages and disadvantages, the cost and the return on investment or, as economists would say, the utility against the disutility have to be balanced." [authors' translation][22]

Guy Braibant's words show to what extent the concept of the public interest had changed by the 1970s.

Therefore, the *Conseil* held that it was appropriate for judges to balance the public interest against harm to private property, financial cost, social disturbance, environmental damage, etc. Hence, because the *Conseil d'État* will make tradeoffs, the primary decision-maker ought to do so as well or risk having its decisions annulled. The 1971 case represents an important acknowledgment by the *Conseil* that public law includes such tradeoffs. This

---

[21] Conseil d'Etat, 28 mai 1971, Ville Nouvelle-Est, Recueil Lebon at. 409.

[22] Prior opinion of the *commissaire de gouvernement* in the case. Braibant, supra at x

jurisprudence is interesting insofar as it is a legal expression of the new concept of the public interest. It is not the only rationale for RIA. In continental Europe, the notion of "quality of the law" was also used to promote the use of RIA.

2. RIA AND QUALITY

It is certain that, because of pressures from the OECD, the development of RIA is closely associated with the notion of quality fostered by better regulation programs.[23]

In the French case,[24] the push for RIA, as explained by Jean Maïa in his book, can be explained by two reasons. The *Conseil d'État* drafted the original 2003 guidelines on Impact Assessment and supported Impact Assessment for draft bills. The motivation was not just to produce better bills, but also to limit the number of new laws. It may seem strange that the quantity of statutes should, in and of itself, be a source of concern as opposed to the burdens of regulatory and tax laws.[25] However, in France the concern is closely tied to debates over the proper role of the legislature vis-à-vis the elite civil service in furthering the public interest.[26] In the view of the *Conseil d'État*, statutes should be

---

[23] See Claudio M. Radaelli (2004): Getting to Grips with Quality in the Diffusion of Regulatory Impact Assessment in Europe, Public Money & Management, 24:5, 271-276. – Maria de Benedetto, Mario Martelli and Nicoletta Rangone, Il Mulino, 2011, p. 23

[24] For Italy see Formez, La qualità della regolamentazione: casi italiani e confronti internazionali, Napoli, 2003 (paper available here: http://www.osservatorioair.it/wp-content/uploads/2009/08/atti_convegno_napoli_ottobre_2003.pdf, last seen 31 March 2013).

[25] The debate in the US has focused not on the mixture of statutes and executive branch rules but rather on the burden on the private sector. For a critique of rulemaking in the United States see THOMAS O. MCGARITY, REINVENTING RATIONALITY: THE ROLE OF REGULATORY ANALYSIS IN THE FEDERAL BUREAUCRACY (1991) at 273.

[26] On the historical roots see Lindseth, *Paradox*, supra at 1404-1407.

general expressions of the public interest and this view permeates debates in France about the number and quality of legislative enactments.[27] The *Conseil d'État* has long lamented the "proliferation of laws", the "overproduction" of norms, and the inflation of rules by parliament and the executive.[28] The *Conseil d'État* argues that the growth in the number of legal texts means a loss of legal value. Law becomes trivialized; *"quand le droit bavarde, le citoyen ne lui prête qu'une oreille distraite"* ("when the law babbles on and on, citizens lend it but a distracted ear"). This multiplication of legal texts may result in a breach of equality before the law, a democratic deficit, and legal insecurity.[29] An interest in halting this "tide" was behind the *Conseil d'État*'s support of IAs for draft laws. The *Conseil* understood the IA requirement as consistent with its own commitment to upholding the public interest.

3. RIA AS A PRODUCT OF AMERICAN ADMINISTRATIVE LAW PRINCIPLES

In the United States, some cases indicate that judicial review under the APA could mandate a mild form of RIA. In US, administrative law independent agencies enjoy broad discretion to

---

[27] Concern with the quality of law is not only French. Research on legal drafting and the quality of law began in Germany and Switzerland in the 19th and 20th century and in the common law world in the 70s. See L. Eck, *Les études d'impact et la légistique*, in LES ÉTUDES D'IMPACT ACCOMPAGNANT LES PROJETS DE LOI, M. PHILIP-GAY (ED.) (2012); K. GILBERT, LA LÉGISTIQUE AU CONCRET : LES PROCESSUS DE RATIONALISATION DU DROIT, Thèse, Paris 2, 2007.

[28] See RAPPORT PUBLIC DU CONSEIL D'ÉTAT 1991 at 15. The principal author of the report was Françoise Chandernagor, a historian and member of the *Conseil d'État*. In 2005, the *Conseil d'État* reported that there were 10, 500 laws and 120, 000 decrees in force. In 1991 the *Conseil d'État* counted 7500 laws. In addition, each year ministries issue more than 10 000 executive orders.

[29] For an analysis of the French definition of legal quality, see C.-H. MONTIN, LEGISTICS AND THE QUALITY OF LEGISLATION IN FRANCE at http://www.montin.com/documents/legistics.pdf

invoke their expertise in balancing competing interests. Nevertheless, this discretion is constrained by the requirements of reasoned decision-making, which means that in cases where parties raise reasonable alternatives to the agency's position, reasoned decision-making requires considering those alternatives. Reasoned decision-making confers upon agencies a duty to bring their expertise and their best judgment to "bear upon that issue".[30]

Through these broad rules of US administrative law, the Courts have "inject[ed] cost-benefit considerations"[31] into the rule making process through the "arbitrary or capricious" test of the APA that requires reasoned decision-making. Reasoned decision-making is a standard imposed by the Supreme Court in the State Farm case.[32] According to this case, when formulating a rule, an agency must "articulate a satisfactory explanation for its action including a rational connection between the facts found and the choice made." The court must also consider whether the agency's decision "[is]based on a consideration of the relevant factors."

In *Chamber of Commerce v. SEC*,[33] "the rule at issue required that mutual fund boards have no less than 75% independent directors and be chaired by an independent director".[34] What is interesting in this case, is that one of the grounds for review in the provisions of the Administrative Procedure Act allows a reviewing court to set aside any agency action that is "arbitrary,

---

[30] 412 F.3d 133, § 37.

[31] Richard G. Stoll, Cost-Benefit Analysis Through the Back Door of «Reasoned Decisionmaking»? 31 ELR 10228.

[32] *Motor Veh. Mfrs. Ass'n v. State Farm Ins.*, 463 U.S. 29 (1983).

[33] *Chamber of Commerce v. SEC*, 412 F.3d 133 (D.C. Cir. 2005).

[34] Paul Rose, Christopher J. Walker, The Importance of Cost-Benefit Analysis in Financial Regulation, Report for U.S. Chamber of Commerce; Law and Capital Markets @ Ohio State, March 2013, p. 29.

capricious, an abuse of discretion, or otherwise not in accordance with law."[35]

The US Court of Appeal held in this case that the SEC's failure to consider an alternative violated the APA. Considering and comparing alternatives is central to the RIA/CBA process of reasoning. The Court is of course conscious of the dangers of such a general ruling and then adds, "...the Commission is not required to consider 'every alternative ... conceivable by the mind of man ... regardless of how uncommon or unknown that alternative' may be". [36] Here, however, two dissenting Commissioners raised an idea for an alternative to the rule in question, which should have been considered then. The Court narrows the scope of its ruling by commenting further that the SEC would be "excused for failing to consider this alternative if it were, for whatever reason, unworthy of consideration".[37] As the "alternative was neither frivolous nor out of bounds" the "Commission therefore had an obligation to consider it".[38]

The Court cites as authority for this decision *Laclede Gas Co. v. FERC.*[39] In this case, the Court of Appeal held that "...where a party raises facially reasonable alternatives to FERC's decision to reject a contested settlement, the agency must either consider those alternatives or give some reason, within its broad discretion over contested settlements."

These cases show that US administrative law mandates a mild form of CBA that consisting in the consideration of alternatives, under the general requirement of reasoned decision-making. These cases show that RIA in the American context can be understood in the light of the adversarial model of policy-making

[35] Administrative Procedure Act 5 U.S.C. § 706(2)(A) (2000).

[36] 412 F.3d 133, § 35.

[37] 412 F.3d 133, § 36.

[38] 412 F.3d 133, § 37.

[39] 873 F.2d 1494, 1498 (D.C.Cir.1989).

that is mandated by the APA. Rule-making procedures in the United States require the agency to publish a notice for the proposed rule and listen to all the interested parties. The emphasis on alternatives that RIA makes can be explained in this context of a very contentious policy-making process, which is unique to the United States. Some writers have even called this model "adversarial legalism".[40] CBA gives agencies an objective way of justifying their project and responding to alternative views.

One can understand therefore, why CBA/RIA appeared in the United States. Because the policy-making process is adversarial and contentious, agencies need a standard to evaluate opposing views, especially as Courts oblige them to justify their choice of option, and thereby ensure democratic legitimacy as well.

4. RIA AND THE BETTER REGULATION PROGRAM

RIA is associated in Europe with the "Better Regulation" programme, which as defined by Julia Black, should be understood as "a pragmatic, flexible and pluralistic approach to regulation involving the use of multiple regulatory techniques and a wider range of regulatory actors to implement a regulatory regime. The fashion is thus to talk of 'decentring' regulation;

---

[40] See Robert A Kagan, Adversarial Legalism: The American Way of Law, Harvard University Press, 2009. The author defines adversarial legalism as "a method of policymaking and dispute resolution characterized by comparatively high degrees of: a) formal legal contestation-disputants and competing interests invoke legal rights, duties, and procedural requirements, backed by the threat of recourse to judicial review or enforcement; b) litigant activism-the gathering and submission of evidence and the articulation of claims is dominated or profoundly influenced by disputing parties or interests, acting primarily through lawyers; c) substantive uncertainty-official decisions, in relative or comparative terms, are variable, unpredictable, and reversible; hence adversarial advocacy can have a substantial impact." (Robert A. Kagan, Do Lawyers Cause Adversarial Legalism--A Preliminary Inquiry, 19 Law & Soc. Inquiry 1 (1994)).

'collaborative governance', 'outsourcing regulation', 'empowering participants'; finding 'complementary mixes' of instruments; 'sequencing instruments' and maximising the opportunities for 'win-win' solutions".[41]

The Better Regulation movement is therefore multifaceted. Baldwin traces back the origins of the movement to the deregulation policies set up by the UK Conservative government and explained in the 1985 White Paper entitled *Lifting the Burden*.[42] In this document, the government explained the "negative effect of regulatory compliance costs on business and the need to deregulate by freeing markets and reducing administrative and legislative burdens".[43]

The "Better Regulation" motto first appeared when the Labour government of Tony Blair came into power. Better Regulation was then a strategy of shifting the debate from deregulation to intelligent, efficient ways of regulation. It was the Third Way response, an attempt at reaching an equilibrium between the Conservative agenda of dismantling government and the old welfare state.

RIA is the key element in the Better Regulation tool kit, in which one will also find: "simplification of administrative processes, consolidation of legislation, plans for the reduction of administrative burdens, use of market-friendly alternatives, risk-based approaches to inspections, regulatory budgets, mandatory consultation standards, sustainability assessments of proposed and existing regulation, and ex post review".[44]

---

[41] Julia Black, Tensions in the regulatory state, Public Law 2007, Spr, 58-73.

[42] DTI, *Lifting the Burden*, Cmnd 9571 (1985).

[43] Robert Baldwin, Is better regulation smarter regulation?, 2005, Aut, 485-511.

[44] C. M. Radaelli (2010), Regulating Rule-Making via Impact Assessment. Governance, 23: 89–108.

III. THE HISTORICAL EVOLUTION OF RIA

The history of RIA can be divided broadly in three steps. The mechanism was developed in the Anglo-American context of the conservative governments of the United States and the United Kingdom (A). The tool was then given a new setting and meaning in the UK in the context of the Third Way (B). After this, the tool spread at the EU level and among EU countries as well as throughout the rest of the world thanks to the recommendations of the OECD (C).

1. THE ANGLO-AMERICAN PERIOD: RIA AS A TOOL FOR DE-REGULATION

Adler and Posner identify three steps in the development of CBA/RIA in the American context. First, CBA appears as with the growth of centralized government in the United States: "In the United States, the New Deal government initiated the use of CBA in 1936, when Congress ordered agencies to weigh the costs and benefits of projects designed for flood control".[45] They cite as an example the Flood Control Act of 1936, which provides that projects should be approved if "the benefits to whomsoever they may accrue are in excess of the estimated costs".[46] Secondly, the rise of Progressivism at the end of the nineteenth century and the beginning of the twentieth century, which argued that the functions of government could be separated into two different tasks:

---

[45] Matthew D. Adler, Eric A. Posner, Rethinking Cost Benefit Analysis 109 Yale L.J. 165.

[46] Flood Control Act of 1 ch. 688, § 1. 49 Stat. 1570, 1570 (codified as amended at 33 U.S.C. § 701a (1994). Another writer have seen first instances of CBA in the River and Harbor Act of 1902 (ch. 1079, § 3, 32 Stat. 331, 372 (1902)): Edward Sherwin, The Cost-Benefit Analysis of Financial Regulation: Lessons from the SEC's Stalled Mutual Fund Reform Effort, Stanford Journal of Law, Business, and Finance, Vol. 12, No. 1, 2006.

"those that involve questions of basic policy and social value and those that are administrative or instrumental in value".[47] Finally, the last step involves the invention of the intellectual tools that are at the basis of CBA, namely the development of modern welfare economics.[48]

Without these three steps, the mechanism could not have been created.[49] The first utilization of CBA is found in during the Nixon Administration, when businesses began to complain about the cost of regulation, mainly in the area of environmental regulation. After several attempts under different subsequent administrations, it is in 1981 with Executive Order 12,291 that agencies were obliged to adopt real CBA. Section 2 of the Order stated:

"In promulgating new regulations, reviewing existing regulations, and developing legislative proposals concerning regulation, all agencies, to the extent permitted by law, shall adhere to the following requirements:

(a) Administrative decisions shall be based on adequate information concerning the need for and consequences of proposed government action;

(b) Regulatory action shall not be undertaken unless the potential benefits to society for the regulation outweigh the potential costs to society;

(c) Regulatory objectives shall be chosen to maximize the net benefits to society;

---

[47] Robert H. Nelson, The Economics Profession and tre Making of Public Policy, 25 J. ECON. LITERATURE 49, 52-54 (1987).

[48] Matthew D. Adler, Eric A. Posner, Rethinking Cost Benefit Analysis 109 Yale L.J. 165.

[49] For a precise historical account of the development of CBA in the United States: A. Renda, Impact Assessment in th EU, The State of the Art and the Art of the State, Centre for European Policy Studies, Brussels, 2006, p. 8-56.

(d) Among alternative approaches to any given regulatory objective, the alternative involving the least net cost to society shall be chosen; and

(e) Agencies shall set regulatory priorities with the aim of maximizing the aggregate net benefits to society, taking into account the condition of the particular industries affected by regulations, the condition of the national economy, and other regulatory actions contemplated for the future."[50]

This statement contains all the elements of CBA: first, evidenced-based regulation requires that all proposals have a basis in adequate information and second, the Executive Order defines a rule of decision-making according to which the benefits of the proposal should outweigh its cost to society as a whole. When the Order specifies "society" it means that regulations should be made in the benefit of society as a whole and not in the benefit of specific members of the public. The quality of CBAs was reviewed by the OIRA (Office of Information and Regulatory Affairs), a body created within the Office of Management and Budget (OMB).

The history of CBA in the United States at that time is not trouble-free. CBA was accused constantly of slowing down the process of regulation and placing its focus on competitiveness, at the expense of other important values such as the environment or health. Some commentators even attributed this progression to the takeover of the White House and the OMB by interest groups.[51]

---

[50] See the Executive order here: http://www.archives.gov/federal-register/codification/executive-order/12291.html.

[51] See the references in A. Renda, Impact Assessment in th EU, The State of the Art and the Art of the State, Centre for European Policy Studies, Brussels, 2006, p. 12, footnote 31: the 1992 Report by the OMB Watch and Public Citizen, Voodoo

The Clinton administration passed Executive Order 12,866 in order to resolve conflicts between OIRA and sponsoring agencies and to promote a new "philosophy" of regulation. Section 1(a) of the Order stipulates that:

"In deciding whether and how to regulate, agencies should assess all costs and benefits of available regulatory alternatives, including the alternative of not regulating. Costs and benefits shall be understood to include both quantifiable measures (to the fullest extent that these can be usefully estimated) and qualitative measures of costs and benefits that are difficult to quantify, but nevertheless essential to consider. Further, in choosing among alternative regulatory approaches, agencies should select those approaches that maximize net benefits (including potential economic, environmental, public health and safety, and other advantages; distributive impacts; and equity), unless a statute requires another regulatory approach."[52]

The philosophy is not completely new and the principles remain unchanged: the idea that agencies should consider the "not regulating" option and the idea that some measures may not be quantifiable seem to be new, but otherwise the philosophy remains unchanged.

In the United Kingdom, as Antony Ogus shows,[53] the first attempt at introducing RIA was in 1986, and it came within a

Accounting: The Toll of President Bush's Regulatory Moratorium; B.D. Friedman, Regulation in the Reagan-Bush Era: The
Eruption of Presidential Influence. Pittsburgh, PA: Pittsburgh University Press, 1995; B. Woodward and D.S. Broder, "Quayle's Quest: Curb Rules, Leave 'No Fingerprints'", Washington Post, 9 January 1992.
[52] See the Executive order here: http://www.reginfo.gov/public/jsp/Utilities/EO_12866.pdf.
[53] See Anthony Ogus's paper in the volume entitled « Regulatory Impact Assessment: A Politico- Economic Perspective ».

more general plan aimed at reforming the culture and operations of the British Administration and at deregulating parts of the economy. The Conservative Government of Margaret Thatcher began with caution, requiring sponsoring administrations to evaluate only the impact of draft regulations on costs incurred by firms to comply with the new rule (also called "Compliance Cost Assessment" or CCA).[54]

The White Paper *Lifting the Burden*s considers that, in order to stem the flow of regulations, a three-pronged approach is required:

  i. "a structural analysis of each new proposal, to be prepared and published by the initiating agency concerned, including a systematic assessment of its impact on business enterprise;

  ii. critical scrutiny of the proposal, in particular of the assessment, by a small task force in central Government with real teeth; and

  iii. regular overviews by the task force of proposals in the pipeline and the scope for eliminating, simplifying or rationalising existing requirement systems".[55]

The British approach is much less comprehensive that the US methodology. Only the impact on business is to be taken into account. The document shows a clear bias against regulation, indeed, not even mentioning that a regulation can give benefits.

---

[54] See White Paper, *Lifting the Burden*, Cmnd 9571, 1985; and *Building Business – Not Barriers*, Cmnd 9794, 1986.

[55] White Paper, *Lifting the Burden*, Cmnd 9571, 1985, p. 34.

2. THE NEW TURN: RIA IN THE CONTEXT OF BETTER REGULATION

A new approach in the United Kingdom came about under the Premiership of Tony Blair. The philosophy of the Third Way that inspired him motivated a departure from the previous bias against regulation. The new approach was to be more comprehensive. The National Audit Office explains the evolution thus:

"As part of their Better Regulation Initiative, the Government introduced regulatory impact assessments in August 1998, to replace compliance cost assessments. The intention was to broaden the focus of regulatory appraisal to make regulatory considerations an integral part of policy making. In addition to explaining the purpose of regulation and examining the risks and the financial costs which regulation imposed on business, departments are also required to analyse benefits, and to consider the overall impact on society."[56]

In this context, RIA becomes a part of a general reform of policy-making called Better Regulation, the principles of which are: proportionality, transparency, consistency, targeting, and accountability. RIA becomes, then, a comprehensive tool aimed at establishing a clear method of policy-making. The criteria were detailed as follows:

---

[56] See *Better Regulation: Making Good Use of Regulatory Impact Assessments*, 15 November 2001, HC 329, 2001-02, p 16.

Purpose and intended effect	Identifies the objectives of the regulatory proposal
Risks	Assesses the risks that the proposed regulations are addressing
Benefits	Identifies the benefits of each option including the "do nothing" option
Costs	Looks at all costs including indirect costs
Securing compliance	Identifies options for action
Impact on small business	Using advice from the Small Business Service
Public consultation	Takes the views of those affected, and is clear about assumptions and options for discussion
Monitoring and evaluation	Establishes criteria for monitoring and evaluation
Recommendation	Summarises and makes recommendations to Ministers, having regard to the views expressed in public consultation[1]

With this, RIA becomes much more comprehensive and much less biased. The philosophy of RIA in the United Kingdom has remained essentially the same.

In the EU context, the first attempts at establishing IAs date back to 1986 under the UK Presidency, with the Business Impact Assessment (BIA). But this mechanism did not work properly and suffered many shortcomings:

"BIAs are often carried out as an ex-post 'paper exercise' on already finalised proposals, leading to significant drawbacks with regard to both the quality of the analysis made and the possibility of feeding the results into the drafting process.

Nor does the existing BIA system properly specify the type of analysis to be carried out. This has led to wide variations in the quality of assessments from one department or unit to another."[57]

The publication of the Mandelkern Report published in 2001, as well as work within the OECD led to a reform of the mechanism. The model of IA introduced by the Commission of that era is wide ranging. As Renda summarizes:

"The new integrated impact assessment (IIA) model introduced in 2002 – which incorporates not only the economic impact, but also the social and environmental impact of the proposals concerned – adopts a 'dual stage' approach. All Commission initiatives proposed for inclusion in the Annual Policy Strategy or the Commission Legislative and Work Programme and requiring some regulatory measure for their implementation – thus including not only regulations and directives, but also white papers, expenditure programmes and negotiating guidelines for the international agreements – must undergo a 'preliminary impact assessment'. Moreover, a selected number of proposals with large expected impact are subjected to a more in-depth analysis called 'extended impact assessment'."[58]

The process is clearly more complex. The categories of potential impacts become more extensive: economic, environmental and social impact have to be taken into account. The process is more complex, with different kinds of projects having to comply

---

[57] Final Report Business Impact Assessment (BIA) pilot project, Lessons Learned and the Way Forward, Enterprise Paper No. 9, DG Enterprise, European Commission, 2002, p. 2.

[58] A. Renda, Impact Assessment in th EU, The State of the Art and the Art of the State, Centre for European Policy Studies, Brussels, 2006, p. 53.

with different kinds of IA. CBA must be used, but not on a systematic basis.[59] The European process of RIA is very complicated and burdensome.

One sees clearly from this historical account how RIA has evolved and has been made more complex over time since the creation of the method in the United States.

3. SPREAD AND NEW MEANINGS: MODELS OF IA

As it often happens with legal transplants, a mechanism can be imported, but to serve a different purpose than the one intended for it in its origin. Comparative analysis has shown that RIA is a tool used for multiple, diverse purposes in Europe. As Radaelli observes:

"RIA is a solution to different problems. In Germany, Sweden, and Italy RIA is perceived as a possible solution to the problem of simplification, in the Netherlands it is associated with the issue of competitiveness, in Denmark and Belgium the link is between RIA and the quality of the business environment. At the EU level, RIA is perceived as a response to the problem of legitimacy deficit in the Community's regulatory system".[60]The objectives are different. Their forms differ as well. In the Anglo-American legal world, at EU level, and also in some countries like the UK, Germany or Spain, IAs are clearly quantitative and aimed at reducing administrative burdens, "red tape" as they say, and at promoting the best regulatory outcome in economic terms. France stands in a sharp contrast with this tradition. In France, IAs do not have as a sole objective an economic assessment. On

---

[59] See Commission Impact Assessment Guidelines (January 2009) at: http://ec.europa.eu/governance/impact/key_docs/key_docs_en.htm

[60] See Claudio M. Radaelli (2005): Diffusion without convergence: how political context shapes the adoption of regulatory impact assessment, Journal of European Public Policy, 12:5, 924-943.

the contrary, in the Organic Law[61] the evaluation of the various impacts of legislative proposals are only one of the objectives of IAs, the main objective seems to be legal in a more broad sense. As the Organic Law provides, IAs should specifically assess:

- "the way the bill dovetails with European legislation in force or being prepared, and its impact on the domestic legal system;
- the status of application of the law at national level in the area(s) covered by the bill;
- the conditions of application over time of the envisaged provisions, the legislative and regulatory texts to be abrogated and the transient measures proposed;
- the conditions of application of the envisaged provisions in the local authorities governed by Articles 73 and 74 of the Constitution, in New Caledonia and in the French South Seas and Antarctic Territories, justifying, where applicable, the adaptations proposed and the absence of application of the provisions to some of these authorities;
- the evaluation of the economic, financial, employment and environmental impact and the financial costs and benefits expected form the provisions envisaged for each category of public administration and natural and legal persons concerned, indicating the calculation method used;
- the evaluation of the consequences of the provisions on public-sector employment;
- the consultations carried out prior to the Council of State being called upon; and
- the provisional list of implementation legislation necessary".[62]

---

[61] In France, Organic Laws are provisions implementing constitutional requirements and having the same legal force as the Constitution.

[62] Loi organique n° 2009-403 du 15 avril 2009 relative à l'application des articles 34-1, 39 et 44 de la Constitution, article 8. The translation comes

This list shows very clearly that, in the French model , the IA is primarily concerned with the legal articulation of norms in time and in space (between the EU, national and local levels), as well as the legal implementation of the envisaged provision. This reflects the spirit in which the reform implementing IAs was made in France. IA was introduced primarily because of the *Conseil d'Etat* (the French administrative Supreme Court) concerns regarding legislative quality. The focus was not primarily on reducing burdens or cutting red tape but on the explosion of legal provision and the necessity to clarify the law. This explains why, at the same time, France chose to codify and simplify many parts of its laws.

In contrast to this objective, the United Kingdom is at the forefront of the better regulation agenda that includes a commitment to IA. The focus is here clearly on economic evaluation, reducing administrative burdens and cutting costs with targets such as reducing burdens by 25%.[63] Furthermore, the fact that the IA is to be presented with a summary sheet encapsulating the monetized costs and benefits of the proposal shows the commitment of the different British Governments to a quantitative conception of IA. The focus here is clearly not on the legal aspects of the regulations.

Following these lines, several other countries have taken up in a similar direction, probably with a lesser emphasis on economics. Spain, for example, has developed a more "managerial" acceptation of IA than France. According to the OECD itself, the Royal Decree 1083/2009 of 3 July 2009, (*Memoria del análisis de impacto normativo*)[64] "is motivated by a strong Better

---

from: OECD, Better Regulation in Europe – France, 2010, at pp. 109-110. See also Jean Maïa's paper.

[63] See OECD, Better Regulation in Europe: United Kingdom 2010, at pp. 14-15.

[64] See Guía Metodológica para la elaboración de la Memoria del Análisis de Impacto Normativo at: http://www.seap.minhap.gob.es/es/areas/funcion_

Regulation rationale, contributing to the pursuit of sustainable development, competitiveness and job creation".[65] In 2009, the Government considered the Decree as "a sign of its commitment to an enhanced RIA system, and 'a point of no return' for developing its overall Better Regulation policy".[66] The spirit of the RIA system in Spain is driven not only by economic concerns but also by legal ones: the IA should also assess the adequacy of the norm with the distribution of competences in Spain between the different levels.

In Germany as well, the goal of IA —that comprises also legislative proposals as well as regulatory ones— is to inform decision-makers and reduce the costs of regulation.[67] The current IA guidelines were designed in 2000 (*Leitfaden zur Gesetzesfolgenabschätzung*) and a comprehensive Handbook (*Handbuch zur Gesetzesfolgenabschätzung*) was also published by the Ministry of the Interior. The process introduced by the 2000 reform establishes

> "three types of analysis that are performed at different stages of the regulatory process:
>
> - a preliminary RIA, aimed at testing whether regulation is necessary as well as identifying and comparing alternatives;
> - a concurrent RIA, which should be used to check whether regulatory measures match and suit the regulatees and the regulatory context; and

publica/iniciativas/impacto_normativo.html.

[65] OECD, Better Regulation in Europe: Spain 2010, at p. 91.

[66] See OECD, Better Regulation in Europe: Spain 2010, at p. 91.

[67] See OECD, Better Regulation in Europe: Germany 2010, at p. 98.

- a retrospective RIA, which seeks to assess whether the regulatory objective were achieved after implementation (i.e. ex post evaluation)".[68]

As described in the OECD report the German IA scheme is very much in line with the Anglo-American system of IA: "The focus is on analyzing the costs as well as the benefits, in both monetary and nonmonetary terms. To assess the economic, ecological and social impacts, a predefined questionnaire (checklist) is used to draw attention to possible effects in all three areas examined. The RIA methodological working aid insists on identifying and evaluating alternatives to regulation, including the option of taking no action (step 4 above). The official conducting the RIA is supposed to refer to the competent Ministry and conduct internal checks, and consult an expert in the field in question for a more in-depth RIA."[69]

IV. CONDITIONS AND METHODS OF RIA

Impact assessment experiences do not fit into one single model. There are in fact strong variations between them, which affect at least the following aspects.

IV.A. From one country to another one, the legal basis on which RIA is ground will vary. At one end of the spectrum, there will be jurisdictions in which RIA is required and organized by statutes, or even by the Constitution. In France, for example, assessment of legislative bills has been made a constitutional obligation, provided for in article 39 of the Constitution, since 2008.

[68] See OECD, Better Regulation in Europe: Germany 2010, at p. 98.
[69] Ibidem, at p. 101.

At the other end, there are systems in which IA is regulated in an informal way, by various types of soft law instruments, like guidelines, guidances, circulars, and the like. This is the case in the United Kingdom, the European Union, and also in Greece, as George Dellis explains. Apparently, this informal handling is more frequent than the more formal one.

What varies, too, from one jurisdiction to another one, is the scope of legal instruments subject to RIA, and both in substantive and organic terms. In many countries -for example, Greece, as George Dellis also explains- IA was initially imposed only on regulation affecting the environment-, before being given a wider impact. In other countries, it was meant to apply directly to all regulatory instruments.

As to the institutional scope of RIA, one essential issue is whether it covers all governmental agencies, or only some of them, whose activity seems more adapted to impact assessment. One side of this issue is raised by systems in which some of the agencies have been voluntarily given a large grade of independence with respect to the government and the parliament. Their independence can make impact assessment a bit delicate to conduct . Thus, in the US, the independent regulatory commissions do not have to abide by the presidential executive orders prescribing cost-benefit analysis. Nevertheless, there are examples of systems in which RIA produced by independent authorities is practiced.[70]

In some countries, RIA is either operated by special bodies, or simply promoted and possibly regulated by special bodies in charge of making sure that it is not avoided, or just artificially practiced. Examples of this are the US Office of Information and Regulatory Affairs –which is part of the presidential Office for

---

[70] Alessandro Natalini, Francesco Sarpi e Giulio Vesperini (a cura di), L'analisi dell'impatto della regolazione, Il caso delle Autorità indipendenti, Carocci editore, 2012

Management and Budget–, the British Better Regulation Executive–which belongs to the Department for Business, Innovation and Skills–, the Italian *Ufficio per l'analisi e la verifica dell'impatto della regolamentazione* –part of the Administration of Prime Minister, the Spanish *Agencia Estatal de Evaluación de las Políticas Públicas y la Calidad de los Servicios* –part of the Ministry of the Treasury and Public Administration–[71], while the Australian government has a special body of regulatory impact officers.[72]

IV.D. RIA is not always constant in its objectives, in its techniques nor in the kind of procedure it follows. Even if its general function is considered in a similar way –to anticipate the likely outcomes of the prepared regulation, in order to check if they correspond to the objectives its drafters have in mind– the actual implementation of RIA is not the same. In some systems, it takes the simple form of cost-benefit analysis or rather an analysis of cost-effectiveness, which requires the determination of the least costly way of attaining a certain outcome. In other systems, RIA has an additional purpose to reduce informational costs for individuals and businesses –this is the case in the Netherlands. In some others, it is oriented towards risk assessment and competition assessment –as in the USA, in Canada, in the United Kingdom, in Australia.[73]

Techniques equally vary, in particular as to the indicators that are used in impact evaluation. However, the development of

[71] Maria de Benedetto, Mario Martelli, Nicoletta Rangone, La qualità delle regole, Il Mulino, 2011, p. 156

[72] M. Cerillo and J.Hertin, Regulatory Impact Analysis in Autralia, Brussels, European Commission Joint Research Centre, 2004

[73] Maria de Benedetto, Mario Martelli, Nicoletta Rangone, La qualità delle regole, p.23

common standards and global indicators has generated a certain level of harmonization, as Martina Conticelli explains.[74]

RIA procedures in general contain a constant guiding line, which Edward Donelan describes as an initial and preliminary assessment, then partial RIAs of the various policy options, concluding with a final overall assessment. Jean Maïa explains that, in the French system, a fourth step exists, in which controls the quality of assessments. In most cases, administrative bodies in charge of RIA follow a precise methodology, elaborated by those who are in charge of the promotion of RIA in the governmental apparatus.

Another aspect in which RIA practices of the various systems show significant differences is the way they are connected to the decision-marking processes. Here, one essential issue is how to ensure that those who have the decisional power will take the RIA into account. In the United Kingdom, pursuant to RIA guidance, the ministers have to sign off at three different steps (consultations, final proposal, and revised proposal) in order to certify that they have taken into consideration the assessments.

Another effective means of ensuring that decision-makers have considered the pros and cons provided by the RIA is to make the RIA reports public –George Dellis mentions that their publication is not compulsory in Greece–, or even more, to require the decisions to be motivated with references to the RIAs.

[74] See also : Giacinto della Cananea and Aldo Sandulli (dir.), Global Standards for Public Authorities, Editoriale Scientifica, 2012 – Kevin Davis, Angelina Fisher, Benedict Kingsbury and Sally Engle Merry (eds), Governance by Indicators. Global Power through Quantification and Rankings, Oxford University Press, Law and Global Governance Series, 2012

V. EFFECTS AND LIMITS OF RIA

The main issue is whether a RIA really affects the content of decisions taken in view of it. This depends on various factors. The most direct factor is whether –or not–the RIA given a normative dimension, i.e., as Anthony Ogus explains, the RIA is treated as more or less determinative for policy purposes. Another factor, already mentioned, is whether the RIA is made public, and if decision-makers are obliged to justify their decisions with reference to the findings of the RIA. In this case, decision makers are obviously less free to deviate from the RIA conclusions. Also important is the fact if the RIA is included or not in procedures that also entail the consultation of advisory bodies, or the participation of the public, where such consultative or participatory processes are required, the chances for the final decision to deviate from what the RIA suggests are higher, simply because more political input is fuelled into the procedure.

Another important issue is the influence RIAs can have on ex post evaluation of decisions, and, in particular, concerning their review by judges. Alberto Alemanno's paper focuses on this question. .He shows that possible encounters between IA results and ex post review can follow two scenarios: direct encounters will occur when IA reports can be challenged before courts for alleged breaches of the rules disciplining RIA, or indirect encounters will arise when an IA report can be invoked in order to challenge the validity of the final act. In fact, up to now, studies only show systems in which marked deficiencies of IA reports render the following decisions illegal and susceptible to annulment by judicial review. Thus, in the French system, insufficient environmental impact assessment is a procedural impropriety which can, per se, lead to the annulment of the final decision.

The contributions gathered in this book clearly show that RIA is not a panacea, and that, in all systems where it is practiced, it shows some deficiencies, or at least suffers from obvious limitations.

Study demonstrates that in order for RIA to reach a minimum level of relevance and efficiency in one particular system, there are many conditions to be met: adequate institutional arrangements and procedural inclusion of the RIAs, sufficiently trained professionals to develop and carry out the assessment process, and so on. Needless to say, these conditions are not easy to achieve.

A crucial issue, then, is the fact that RIA is based mainly on economic rationales, which are often not sufficient to assess multi-faceted political decisions. It appears, at least, that some policies are less susceptible to be reduced to a purely economic decision than others, while some policies include too many potential long-run impacts to be easily subject to RIA. Susan Rose-Ackerman mentions climate change, nuclear accidents risks, and the preservation of biodiversity. Anthony Ogus also points out how it is difficult to cope with the uncertainty that affects most of scientific predictions. For these reasons, and for others that will appear in the next chapters, RIA is never a solution to all problems concerning the rationality of regulatory decisions. Nevertheless, as Anthony Ogus concludes, *that does not undermine… its importance: it provides a useful discipline for policy makers, rendering transparent the reasoning which motivates the proposal and systematizing the decision-making process*.

REFERENCES

ADLER M. & POSNER E., *New Foundations of Cost Benefit Analysis* (Harvard Univ. Press. 2006)

ALEMANNO, A., "The Better Regulation Initiative at the Judicial Gate – A Troian Horse within the Commission's walls or the way forward?", *European Law Journal*, 2009, n°15, p. 382 Assemblée Nationale, Les études d'impact et l'élaboration de la loi: rapport d'information sur les critères de contrôle des études d'impact accompagnant les projets de loi (Paris, 2009).

BECKER, H. A., *Social impact assessment: Method and experience in Europe, North America and the developing world*, UCL Press (London and Bristol, Pa 1997).

MARIA DE BENEDETTO, Mario Martelli and Nicoletta Rangone, *La qualità delle regole*, Il Mulino, 2011

BRINKMANN H., Ernst T., Frick F., Koop A., Riedel H., «Comment réduire les lourdeurs bureaucratiques: l'application du modèle des coûts standards en Allemagne», *Revue française d'administration publique*, n°135, 2010, 619-642.

CAROLINE CECOT, Robert Hahn, Andrea Renda, Lorna Schrefles, "An Evaluation of the Quality Assessment in the European Union with Lessons from the US and the EU", *Regulation and Governance*, n°2, p. 494

GEORGE DORAN, "There'a S.M.A.R.T. Way to Write Management's Goals and Objectives", *Management Review*, 1981, n°70, p. 29.

"DOSSIER SUR LES POLITIQUES PUBLIQUES ET L'ÉVALUATION D'IMPACT SUR LA SANTÉ", *Télescope*, vol. 14, n° 2, 2008, printemps-été, p. 1-117.

"EUROPEAN COURT OF AUDITORS, Impact Assessments in the EU Institutions: Do They Support Decision-Making?" (*Special report* No 3, 2010)

DANIEL FABER, *Rethinking the Role of Cost-Benefit Analysis*, The University of Chicago Law Review, 2009, n°73, p. 1361.

HAMPTON P., *Reducing Administrative Burdens: Effective Inspection and Enforcement* (London, 2005).

HAHN R. & LITAN R., "Counting Regulatory Benefits and Costs: Lessons for the US and Europe", *AEI -Brookings* 04-07.

House of Lords, "European Union Committee, Fourth Report, Impact Assessments in the EU: room for improvement?" (Sessions 2009-2010)

Scott Jacobs, *Current Trends in Regulatory Impact Analysis: The Challenges of Mainstreaming RIA into Policy-Making*, Jacobs and Associates, 2006

Kirkpatrick C., Parker D., *Regulatory impact assessment: towards better regulation?*, CRC series on competition, regulation and development (Edward Elgar, 2008).

Antonio La Spina and Ginadomenico Majone, *Lo Stato Regolatore*, il Mulino, 2000

Lasserre B., *Méthodologie des études d'impact et coût de la règlementation: rapport du groupe de travail* (mars 2004).

Luzius Mader, "Evaluating the Effects: A Contribution to the Quality of Legislation", *Statute Law Review*, 2001, p. 119

Bernardo Mattarella, *La trappola delle leggi*, Il Mulino, 2011

Meuwese A.C., *Impact Assessment in EU Law Making* (Kluwer, 2008).

OECD, *L'analyse de l'impact de la réglementation: Meilleures pratiques dans les pays de l'OCDE* (1997)

OECD (2007), Stéphane Jacobzone, Gregory Bounds, Chang-Won Choi et Claire Miguet, «Regulatory Management Systems across OCDE countries: Indicators of Recent Achievements and Challenges», Paris, *Documents de travail de l'OCDE sur la gouvernance publique*, n° 9, Paris

OECD, *L'analyse d'impact de la réglementation: un outil au service de la cohérence des politiques* (2009)

Robert Pildes and Cass Sunstein, "Reinventing the Regulatory State", *The University of Chicago Law Review*, 1995, n°62, p. 1

Claudio Radaelli (ed.), *L'analisi d'impatto della regolazione in prospettiva comparata*, Rubettino, 2001

Radaelli, C. M., 'The diffusion of regulatory impact analysis in OECD countries: best practices or lesson-drawing?', *European Journal of Political Research*, 43(5): 2004, 725-749.

Radaelli, C. M., 'Diffusion without convergence: How political context shapes the adoption of regulatory impact assessment', *Journal of European Public Policy*, 12(5): 2005, 924-843.

RADAELLI C. M. & MEUWESE A.C., 'Hard Questions, Hard Solutions: Proceduralisation through Impact Assessment in the EU", *West European Politics*, 33(1): 2010, 136-153.

RENDA A., *Impact Assessment in the EU – The State of the Art and the Art of the State* (Centre for European Policy Studies, Brussels, 2006).

REVESZ R. & LIVERMORE M., *Retaking Rationality: How Cost Benefit Analysis Can Better Protect the Environment and Our Health* (Oxford Univ. press, 2008)

ROBERTSON, C., "Impact assessment in the European Union", *Eipascope*, n° 2, 2008, 17-20

SÉNAT, "Projet de loi organique relatif á l'application des articles 34-1, 39 et 44 de la Constitution: rapport de M Jean-Jacques Hyest" (02/2009)

SUNSTEIN C., *The Cost Benefit State : The Future of Regulatory Protection* (2003, Administrative ABA)

VERSCHUUREN J., *The Impact of Legislation – A critical Analysis of Ex Ante Evaluation* (Martinus Nijhoff Pub., 2009).

SIMON WEATHERILL (ED.), *Better Regulation*, Hart Publishing, 2007

WILLIAM WEST, "Administrative Rulemaking: An Old and Emerging Litterature", *Public Administration Review*, 2005, n°65, p.655

WISMAR M., Blau J., Ernst K., Figueras J., Eds. *The Effectiveness of Health Impact Assessment: Scope and limitations of supporting decision-making in Europe. Copenhagen: European Observatory on Health Systems and Policies*, World Health Organization, 2007.

ZERBE JR., R.O., 'Is Cost-Benefit Analysis legal? Three Rules', *Journal of Policy Analysis and Management*, vol. 17:1998, 419-456.

CHAPTER II

REGULATORY IMPACT ASSESSMENT: A POLITICO-ECONOMIC PERSPECTIVE

ANTHONY OGUS*

* Emeritus Professor, University of Manchester. Erasmus Professor Fundamentals of Private Law, University of Rotterdam.

CONTENTS

I. INTRODUCTION: GROWTH AND EXPANSION OF RIA 55

II. SOME IMPORTANT PRACTICAL LIMITS TO COST-BENE-
FIT 57

III. DISCOUNTING FOR THE FUTURE 59

IV. VALUING NON-MARKETABLE RESOURCES 59

V. THE NORMATIVE DIMENSION 61

VI. RISK MANAGEMENT; RISK AVERSION AND IRRATIONAL
RISK PERCEPTIONS 63

VII. DEALING WITH UNCERTAINTY 65

VIII. THE COST-EFFECTIVENESS ALTERNATIVE 67

IX. CONCLUSIONS: THE POLITICAL DIMENSION 68

REFERENCES 70

"Regulatory Impact Assessment: A Politico-Economic Perspective": Some Comments on Professor Ogus' Paper From
a Law and Economics Point of View,
FRÉDÉRIC MARTY. 73

I. INTRODUCTION: GROWTH AND EXPANSION OF RIA

T HE scrutiny of regulatory proposals to predict their impact and consequences has been variously referred to as 'regulatory impact analysis', 'regulatory impact assessment' and 'regulatory impact appraisal' (all conveniently using the same acronym RIA), the differences between the various labels reflecting perhaps different degrees of robustness. Whereas 'analysis' implies something scientific and rigorous, 'assessment' and 'appraisal' carries connotations of a looser, broad-brush approach.

RIA has become an important tool of modern government (Radaelli, 2004). Its increasing use reflects perceptions which became widespread in the last decade of the 20th century that much regulation was disproportionate or ill-targeted; and even where the intervention was appropriate, the same outcome could be achieved by cheaper means. In many areas where it is applied, RIA also draws inspiration from the phenomenon of risk assessment which has become such an important part of management in both the private and public sectors (Hood et al, 2001).

In different countries, RIA has taken different forms (OECD, 2009). In its weakest form, it has come to mean no more than that regulatory policymakers must take a hard look at regulatory policy proposals and their likely impact, if implemented. Policymakers may perhaps be required to respond to a checklist of questions such as: can the regulatory requirements be effectively enforced? Can those affected by the requirements adequately understand them? But increasingly, in developed countries, it has implied the use of cost-benefit, or cost-effectiveness, analysis in a more or less rigorous manner; and it is on these approaches that I shall focus.

The principal model for the cost-benefit approach to RIA has been that developed in the USA, notably under Robert Reagan's Executive Order 12,291 (Heimann et al, 1990). Apart from indicating what data, relating to proposed regulatory reform, was to be collected and how it was to be analysed, this crucially prescribed that '[r]egulatory action shall not be undertaken unless the potential benefits to society outweigh the potential costs to society' (EO 12,291, §2(b)). Under the Clinton Administration, the principles and procedures remained largely intact, but there were some changes of emphasis, notably that the benefits of the intended measure should 'justify' the costs, rather than 'outweigh' them, and that regard should be had to 'distributive impacts; and equity' (EO 12,866, §1). Subsequent American Administrations, including that of Barack Obama, have continued to operate the system under EO 12,866.

Other jurisdictions were slower to adopt RIA. The UK system of appraisal evolved into a cost-benefit approach in 1996 (Froud et al, 1998), and in 2001 14 out of 28 OECD countries were reported as using RIA comprehensively and a further six as using it selectively (Radaelli, 2004, 723). In Europe, the key development took place in 2005 when the Commission introduced its own system. As modified in 2009 (European Commission, 2009), the guidelines require the relevant department to assess against the baseline the likely impact of reform proposals in qualitative, and, if possible, quantitative and monetary terms. Under the concept of 'proportionate level of analysis', the depth of the analysis should reflect the importance of the proposal and the seriousness of its likely impact. Special attention is to be given to the impact on small business enterprises; and, as regards distributional justice, estimates are expected of impacts on different social and economic groups and on existing inequalities.

In this paper, I shall not be concerned to examine the details of the methods and procedures used in the EU and elsewhere; nor to attempt any evaluation of the effectiveness of the systems (on this, see Cecot et al, 2008; and Wiener and Alemmano, 2010). Instead, at a general level, I shall explore what economic appraisal of legislative proposals can, and cannot achieve, and the political implications of these limitations; in short where economics stops and political debate begins. To do this, I start with the general recognition that RIA cannot provide a determinative test of whether a particular proposal should be implemented. Its value lies rather in providing some (relatively) systematic information for policymakers (Posner, 2001), rendering transparent the regulatory process and imposing an important discipline on officials preparing policy proposals, forcing them to address key questions in a coherent manner (Froud et al, 1998). To understand the reasons for this, we must examine, first, the practical limits to the cost-benefit approach and, then, the political nature of some of its features.

II. SOME IMPORTANT PRACTICAL LIMITS TO COST-BENEFIT

Although the basic idea of cost-benefit analysis (CBA), estimating the costs and benefits of particular proposals and comparing them, is relatively simple, much depends on the particular context. CBA as a policy instrument was developed in the 1930s for the purpose of evaluating the appropriateness of public projects such as, in the USA, flood water defences and, in the UK, the siting of the Third London Airport (Dasgupta and Pearce, 1972, 11-13).

Within such a context, one should not underestimate the complexity of assessing the costs and benefits of the states of the world with and without the proposed action, but the character of the exercise in relation to such projects is generally unproblematic: the public agency undertakes the action and the first-order changes to the state of the world (e.g. the compulsory purchase of land) are largely predictable. The making of a regulation is not 'action' in the same sense; it is rather the promulgation of a norm which policymakers hope will lead to the intended outcome (Ogus, 1998). This nuance affects CBA in at least two important ways. First, since it does not follow that behaviour will necessarily change in the intended way, some estimate must be made of the level of predicted compliance and this will be a function of, *inter alia*, the resources committed to enforcement. Secondly, attention has to be directed to the causal relationship between the law and the desired outcome, and to the counterfactual, that the desired outcome may occur for other reasons.

Another problematic dimension relates to the scope of the effects being considered. It may be unrealistic to attempt to measure the impact of the proposed measure on markets other than those relevant to the regulated activity, but even within that narrower framework some indirect effects may be generated which though not unimportant will tend to be ignored. For example, raising quality standards and therefore the price of one type of product may cause some demand to shift to a near-equivalent, but less-regulated, product with perhaps no reduction in damage costs. And suppliers may seek to recoup compliance costs by reducing quality, in other, perhaps less observable aspects of the production process.

In short, we must recognise that in practice CBA provides a far from complete analysis of the costs and benefits likely to arise from a regulatory proposal. We must also be sensitive to the fact that some aspects of the process necessarily involve political judgement. I will now seek to identify those aspects.

III. DISCOUNTING FOR THE FUTURE

The impact in some areas of regulation, for example those dealing with ecological phenomena, takes places over an extended timescale. In consequence, a present value has to be given to costs and benefits which will accrue only in the future, perhaps several centuries away. The problems that this poses for CBA feature prominently in Susan Rose-Ackerman's paper in this collection (Rose-Ackerman, 2011) and I need here only refer to the fact that there is little consensus among economists and others as to how to select an appropriate social discount rate. The balancing of future benefits against current costs thus becomes essentially a matter for political judgement.

IV. VALUING NON-MARKETABLE RESOURCES

A familiar criticism of CBA as applied to regulatory proposals is that the costs, notably compliance costs, of regulatory intervention are typically easier to quantify than the benefits and, for that reason, tend to dominate the analysis, and bias the process against regulation (Ackerman and Heinzerling, 2004). Quantification is particularly difficult where the regulatory proposals aim to protect non-marketable assets, such as the life, health and safety of human beings or the environment. Economists have developed relatively sophisticated techniques for monetarising these benefits, based on willingness to pay (Heyes, 2007). These techniques might be either hypothetical – using questionnaires to discover what individuals would be willing to pay for increased safety or an improved environment – or actual – derived from regression analysis of differentials in earnings between riskier and safer jobs and differentials in property prices between environmentally more and less attractive areas, or the travel costs which people are willing to pay to visit the former.

It is relatively easy to criticise these methods of quantification (e.g., McGarity 1991). A hypothetical question such as 'what additional price would you would be prepared to pay for your air tickets to reduce the risk of a fatal accident from one in one hundred thousand to one in a million?' may not be very meaningful to many to whom it is addressed, and answers may not, in any event, be reliable because respondents are not actually having to pay anything. Then, as regards statistical analysis of actual decisions, adequate data for all relevant variables are difficult to obtain.

But even if that were not the case, evaluations of this kind can give rise to political difficulties. In the first place, the very fact of attributing a price to human life can generate hostility from people who are suspicious of policies which 'sacrifice lives' for profits. It is not difficult for the media to present this as another example of 'wicked capitalism'. (see, e.g., *The Socialist* 12 July 2002). Such a response is irrational insofar as it fails to recognise that all safety policies inevitably place a price on human life and limb, however large that might be. Thus, although government departments, regulatory institutions and firms which engage in a cost-benefit appraisal of safety measures may prefer not to render explicit the value that they attribute to the saving of a statistical life, this is a vital function of RIA and one on which transparency is important (Viscusi and Aldy, 2003).

Other political difficulties may arise from differentiating between types of lives. If willingness to pay is the basis of the evaluation, then the value of a life will reflect the wealth of the relevant individual, with the politically awkward implication that more ought to be paid to save the life of a rich individual than that of a pauper. Now, although all wo(men) may be equal in the sight of God, they are not equal in the real world and richer people will pay more than poorer people for their own health and safety (Sunstein, 2004a). If regulatory interventions are, then, to mimic market behaviour, there will be divergences in the value of a statistical life so that, for example, the safely level of taxis will be higher than that of buses, the differential cost being reflected in the respective fares. Conversely, a redistributional policy may be pursued by attributing, for example, a common value to life across regulatory programmes, but that policy will be effective only if poorer beneficiaries of the programmes pay less than their richer counterparts for the elevated standard (Sunstein, 2004a).

Analogously, it has to be decided whether different values should be attributed according to the age of the people at risk: Should the safety of children be given preference over that of elderly people, irrespective of market considerations based on willingness to pay? Here ethical considerations may suggest a positive answer, since 'every old person was once young, and … if all goes well, young people will eventually be old' (Sunstein, 2004b). But again, attention has to be given to how the burden of the regulatory burden is discharged.

To summarise: politically difficult decisions have to be made as to whether to attribute a common value to life across regulatory programmes and irrespective of the wealth and age of the individuals at risk.

V. THE NORMATIVE DIMENSION

The Reagan version of RIA came close to treating the cost-benefit outcome as determinative for policy purposes. Contemporary advocates of the system might be less dogmatic, but they assume that RIA provides a strong signal of what should be regarded as desirable (Hahn, 2010). The normative dimension of cost-benefit analysis, however, remains problematic.

Cost-benefit analysis, as typically used, simply compares the aggregate gains to be secured by the regulatory intervention against aggregate losses. As such, it reflects the Kaldor-Hicks criterion of allocative efficiency improvements (aggregate gains exceeding aggregate losses) and suffers from the familiar weaknesses of that concept as a normative criterion. Most importantly, the approach allows losses to be imposed on some individuals or groups, for the purpose of generating benefits for the community as a whole. Now it may be that, in general, many, perhaps most, people would regard regulatory policies satisfying the Kaldor-Hicks test to be preferable to those which have to satisfy the alternative criterion of Pareto efficiency improvements (some gains and no losers), since the latter blocks all interventions which generate some losses to some individuals in the community. But, presumably, such a preference would have important limits.

It is impossible to define with any precision what those limits might be. We can of course attempt to speculate and that might lead us to have regard to something like the following considerations (Ogus, 2004). First, the size of the aggregate costs relative to the aggregate benefits: the smaller the former, the more acceptable the intervention. Secondly, identification of the groups within the community which benefit and lose respectively from the activity which imposes the costs. The more that these groups overlap, the more acceptable the intervention. Thirdly, the extent to which the costs are spread over the community at large: the more narrowly focused, and identifiable, the losers, the more unacceptable the intervention.

Given the vagueness of these guidelines, resort to political decision-making is inevitable. And the same applies to other distributional dimensions, for example if there is a perception that the intervention would unduly benefit richer people at the expense of poorer people. It may be possible to devise some form of weighting to deal with this contingency (Frank and Sunstein,

2001), but agreement would still have to be reached on what weighting to apply.

Several systems of RIA, including those operating in the USA and the EU, require analysts to provide some indication of distributional impact. The impression gained by those who have surveyed the systems in practice is, however, that little serious attention is given to this dimension by those preparing the analysis (Radaelli, 2004). This may result from difficulties in determining the relative impact of proposals on different socio-economic groups, but the more likely explanation is a fear that rendering the system too transparent in terms of distributional outcomes will render it vulnerable to political manipulation.

VI. RISK MANAGEMENT; RISK AVERSION AND IRRATIONAL RISK PERCEPTIONS

The application of RIA and cost-benefit analysis to risk assessment and risk management is in principle straightforward. If the cost to society of an unabated risk is pD, where p is the probability of the unwanted event and D the amount of loss if the risk materialises, then the economic goal is to minimise $C_1 + C_2 + pD$, where C_1 are the costs of taking precautions which reduce pD and C_2, the administrative costs of the regulatory instrument necessary to ensure that the relevant precautions are taken (Calabresi, 1970).

However, problems often arise, and political considerations thus intrude, because social psychology studies have shown that ordinary individuals' perceptions of risk diverge from the scientific predictions of pD (Noll and Krier, 2000), leading to a demand for regulatory responses significantly different from that which would otherwise emerge from the RIA. In particular, ordinary people:

- over-estimate risks identical, or analogous, to those arising from events receiving much media attention (availability heuristic) – so, for example, the newsworthiness of a major accident will make people think that the likelihood of the risk recurring is much greater than its objective probability;
- over-estimate risks which have already materialised (hindsight bias) – ex post awareness distorts ex ante appreciation;
- over-value the benefit of preventing (or reducing) risks from new activities or technologies (status quo bias) – newly created risks are thought to be more dangerous than those we are accustomed to.

To what extent should policymakers adjust safety regulation upwards to meet the preferences implicit in these perceptions? Let us, first, acknowledge the strength of a simple argument, provided by mainstream welfare economics, for meeting assumed lay preferences. Since the object of economic decision-making is to maximise utility, risk-aversion, where it exists, must be taken into account as an important part of individual preferences. Even if the lay perceptions of risk outlined above are 'irrational', they cause disutility in the form of real fear and anxiety and therefore there is a justification in making safety policy meet standards higher than those required by expert assessments (Adler, 2004).

Adopting this approach literally would, however, lead to disproportionate responses to flawed and irrational risk perceptions and seriously inhibit technological development (Viscusi, 1998). Nor does economic reasoning ineluctably lead to such a conclusion. The seminal work of Ronald Coase teaches us to be sceptical of normative propositions that the *active* creators of risks should always be expected to modify their conduct (Coase, 1960). In some situations the potential victims can reduce, or adapt to, the risk at lower cost. If, and to the extent that, attitudes to risk are based on inadequate information or fallacious understanding, it can be argued that the disutility to which these give rise may more easily and cheaply be contained by the better informing and educating of public opinion (Sunstein, 2002).

Another line of reasoning which points in the same direction can be derived from the concept of 'moral hazard', familiar in the context of insurance. If policymakers were to respond to all instances of phobia generated by risks, that would create disincentives for individuals to master such phenomena; it might also exacerbate the problem by 'legitimising' irrational public reactions and thereby adding to the anxiety (Chang, 2004).

VII. DEALING WITH UNCERTAINTY

We are becoming increasingly aware, through such phenomena as global warming and genetically modified crops, that scientific predictions are subject to uncertainty. Because an insufficient degree of protection against some of these risks can generate huge welfare losses, there is much public anxiety and pressure on governments to take preventative action. This has led to the articulation of a 'precautionary principle' and its endorsement in a number of international and national instruments (de Sadeleer, 2002).

The precautionary principle remains ambiguous but has been interpreted to mean that where serious and irreversible damage can result, the need for protection should supersede economic considerations.[1] Such a response is untenable because 'there is no escape from evaluation: whatever rule we adopt it will imply an economic value' (Pearce, 1994); and it cannot be the case that society is prepared to devote an infinite amount of resources to prevent the materialisation of any given risk, let alone a specu-

---

[1] See, e.g., the decision of the European Court of Justice in *Pfizer Animal Health v Council* 2002, T-13/99, para. 456.

lative risk. Cost-benefit analysis does not generally involve the assessment of costs on an opportunity-cost basis, but here the concept is of great significance: it makes us aware that efforts to prevent certain risks may lead to worse outcomes, because fewer resources are then available to deal with other risks (Majone, 2002). For example, if we spend large amounts on removing from hospitals minute risks of salmonella, we have less money available to use elsewhere in healthcare, leading to a loss of lives more serious than that posed by the risk of salmonella.

Another, striking illustration is provided by the Hatfield railway disaster of 2000, which led to popular demands in Britain for an improvement in the safety of railway tracks. The government response was to insist on emergency work which created considerable delays on train services and induced many potential passengers to travel by road rather than by rail. Since the risks of death or serious injury from a road accident were significantly higher than those arising from railway travel even on the unrepaired lines, this probably resulted in higher accident costs, and a net loss to social welfare (Economist, 2000).

It is, of course, true that scientific uncertainty creates dilemmas for risk management, but unnecessary difficulties are imposed on policymakers if particular risks are singled out for particular treatment, relying on the existence of uncertainty. It is wrong artificially to distinguish between those risks as to which we have sufficient information to undertake a cost-benefit justified risk management and those risks where we do not have such information: 'in reality, these are two points on a knowledge-ignorance continuum rather than two qualitatively distinct situations' (Majone, 2002). Scientific uncertainty indeed attaches to all risks and we must do the best we can in the face of it.

VIII. THE COST-EFFECTIVENESS ALTERNATIVE

Formal systems of impact assessment sometimes suggest or require cost-effectiveness analysis rather than cost-benefit analysis. Compared to the latter, cost-effectiveness analysis is a less ambitious mode of economic appraisal (see generally Levin and McEwan, 2000). It has two principal functions: to determine the type of intervention which will maximise benefits for a given level of costs, specified by policy-makers; and to determine what intervention will generate specified benefits at lowest cost. The fact that benefits are, generally, more difficult to quantify than costs means that the second function is more frequently encountered.

The EU guidelines for RIA show how cost-effectiveness analysis can complement cost-benefit analysis: 'This method should be used when your initiative consists of a fixed objective (a certain level or target to be realised by a given date). It requires calculating the cost needed to achieve the objective, and then comparing the costs of the different options. It is an alternative to cost-benefit analysis in cases where it is difficult to value benefits in money terms. Cost-effectiveness analysis results in a ranking of regulatory options based on 'cost per unit of effectiveness' of each measure' (EU, 2009).

This guidance contains, in fact, two ideas which are different, though related. On the one hand, there are cases where the benefits of the intervention are difficult or impossible to quantify but by guesswork, intuition or otherwise, the proposal is treated as satisfying the cost-benefit test, and thus, in normative economic terms, is Kaldor-Hicks efficient. On the other hand, there are interventionist measures which do not, or cannot, pass the cost-benefit test but which nevertheless governments are determined to introduce for other reasons, perhaps on grounds of distributional justice. Some transfer payments, such as grants or allowances, come into this category since what is transferred might have the same value to the recipient as to the transferor, and thus generate no benefits, while the transfer itself is costly (Posner, 2004).

More generally, cost-effectiveness analysis has an important role to play in relation to legal interventions which are regarded as desirable politically and which do not aim at allocative efficiency. Too often, those engaging in economic analysis of law have regarded the scrutiny of such measures as outside their ambit, because they have been too obsessed with advocating efficient outcomes. As such, they have missed a major opportunity for exploiting their talents. Eric Posner puts the matter succinctly: 'even if politically motivated transfers are regrettable, they are a fact of life, and it is an important task to analyze how to implement them in a way that minimizes their disruptive impact on the economy' (Posner, 2004).

IX. CONCLUSIONS: THE POLITICAL DIMENSION

It remains to draw some brief conclusions from the preceding discussion. The first of these is obvious. Given its limitations in terms both of the problematic normative implications and of the speculative character of the data which must be invoked for some aspects of the analysis, the cost-benefit assessment at the heart of RIA cannot provide a determinative indicator of whether a given set of legislative proposals is desirable. That does not, nevertheless, undermine its importance: it provides a useful discipline for policymakers, rendering transparent the reasoning which motivates the proposal and systematising the decision-making process.

Throughout this paper, I have indicated that the technical exposition of cost-benefit analysis cannot be divorced from a political input, whether this relates to what is acceptable from a perspective of distributional justice or ethical judgements; or the extent to which concessions should be made to public opinion on, for example, risks, where this differs from the conclusions emerging from the RIA process.

This raises questions relating to the institutional arrangements for RIA, in particular, to what extent the technical economic analysis should be integrated with the appraisal of the more open-ended issues to which RIA necessarily gives rise; and consequently what arrangements, if any, should be made for public consultation during the RIA process. But these are questions which can best be addressed by administrative lawyers and political scientists.

REFERENCES

ACKERMAN, F. and L. Heinzerling (2004). *Priceless: On Knowing the Price of Everything and Value or Nothing*, New York: New Press.

ADLER, M.D. (2004), 'Fear Assessment: Cost-Benefit Analysis and the Pricing of Fear and Anxiety', *Chicago-Kent Law Review*, 77: 977-1054.

CALABRESI, G.(1970). *The Cost of Accidents: A Legal and Economic Analysis*. New Haven: Yale University Press.

CECOT, C., Hahn, R., Renda, A. and Schrefler, L. (2008), 'An evaluation of the quality of impact assessment in the European Union with lessons for the US and the EU', *Regulation and Governance*, 2: 405-424.

CHANG, H.F. (2004). 'Risk Regulation, Endogenous Public Concerns, and the Hormones Dispute: Nothing to Fear but Fear Itself?' *Southern California Law Review*, 77: 743-776.

COASE, R.H. (1960) 'The Problem of Social Cost', *Journal of Law and Economics*, 3: 1-44.

DASGUPTA, A.K. and D.W. Pearce (1972). *Cost-Benefit Analysis: Theory and Practice*. London: Macmillan.

ECONOMIST, The (2000), 'How Not To Run A Railway', 23 November.

EUROPEAN COMMISSION (2009), *Impact Assessment Guidelines*, SEC (2009) 92.

FRANK, R.H and C.R Sunstein (2001). 'Cost-Benefit Analysis and Relative Position', *University of Chicago Law Review*: 68:323-374.

FROUD, J., R. Boden, A. Ogus, and P. Stubbs (1998). *Controlling the Regulators*, Basingstoke: Macmillan.

HAHN, R.W.(2010). 'Designing Smarter Regulation with Improved Benefit-Cost Analysis', *Journal of Benefit-Cost Analysis* 1(1), Article 5..

HEIMANN, C.M. et al. (1990). 'Project: The Impact of Cost-Benefit Analysis on Administrative Law,' *Administrative Law Review*, 42: 545-654.

HEYES, A. (2007). 'Evaluating environmental laws and regulation: methods and controversies' in M.T. de Almeida (ed.), *Legislative Evaluation*, Lisbon: National Institute of Administration, 127-137.

HOOD, C., H. Rothstein and R. Baldwin (2001). *The Government of Risk: Understanding Risk Regulation Regimes*, Oxford; Oxford University Press.

LEVIN, H.M. and McEwan, P.J. (2000). *Cost-Effectiveness Analysis* (2nd edn), Thousand Oaks: Sage Publications.

MAJONE, G. (2002). 'What Price Safety? The Precautionary Principle and its Policy Implications', *Journal of Common Market Studies*, 40: 89-109.

MCGARITY, T. (1991). *Reinventing Rationality: The Role of Regulatory Analysis in the Federal Bureaucracy*, Cambridge: Cambridge University Press.

NOLL, R.G. and J.E. Krier (2000), 'Some Implications of Cognitive Psychology for Risk Regulation' in C. Sunstein (ed.), *Behavioral Law and Economics* Cambridge: Cambridge University Press.

OECD (2009). *REGULATORY IMPACT ANALYSIS: A TOOL FOR POLICY COHERENCE*, Paris: OECD.

OGUS, A. (1998). 'Regulatory Appraisal: A Neglected Opportunity for Law and Economics', *European Journal of Law and Economics*, 6: 53-68.

OGUS, A. (2004). 'Risk Management from an Economic Perspective' in E. Vos and G. van Calster (eds.), *Risico en voorzorg in de rechtsmaatschappij*, Mortsel: Intersentia, 229-238.

PEARCE, D.S. (1994). 'The Precautionary Principle and Economic Analysis' in T. O'Riordan and J. Cameron (eds.) *Interpreting the Precautionary Principle*, London: Cameron and May.

POSNER, E. (2001). 'Controlling Agencies with Cost-Benefit-Analysis: A Positive Political Theory Perspective', *University of Chicago Law Review*, 68: 1137-1199.

POSNER, E. (2004). 'Transfer Regulations and Cost-Effectiveness Analysis', *Duke Law Journal*, 53: 1067-1110.

RADAELLI, C.M. (2004). 'The Diffusion of Regulatory Impact Analysis – Best Practice or Lesson-Drawing', *European Journal of Political Research*, 43: 723-747.

ROSE-ACKERMAN, S. (2011). 'Putting Cost-Benefit Analysis in its Place: Rethinking Regulatory Review'

SADELEER, N. de (2002). *Environmental Principles: From Political Slogans to Legal Rules*, Oxford, Oxford University Press.

SOCIALIST, The (2002). 'Bring Rail Bosses to Justice', *The Socialist*, 12 July.

SUNSTEIN, C.R. (2002). *Risk and Reason: Safety, Law, and the Environment* Cambridge: Cambridge University Press.

SUNSTEIN, C.R. (2004a). 'Are Poor People Worth Less Than Rich People? Disaggregating the Value of Statistical Lives', *AEI-Brookings Working Paper Working Paper 04-5.*

SUNSTEIN, C.R. (2004b). 'Lives, Life-Years and Willingness to Pay', *Columbia Law Review*, 104: 205-251. X. -IX. -

VISCUSI, W.K. (1998). Rational Risk Policy, Oxford: Clarendon Press.

WIENER, J.B. and Alemmano, A. (2010). 'Comparing Regulatory Oversight Bodies across the Atlantic: The Office of Information and Regulatory Affairs in the US and the Impact Assessment Board in the EU' in S.Rose-Ackerman and P.L. Lindseth (eds.), Comparative Administrative Law, Cheltenham: Edward Elgar, Chap. 19.

"REGULATORY IMPACT ASSESSMENT: A POLITICO-ECONOMIC PERSPECTIVE": SOME COMMENTS ON PROFESSOR OGUS' PAPER FROM A LAW AND ECONOMICS POINT OF VIEW

FRÉDÉRIC MARTY*

T HE paper presented by Professor Ogus expounds the origins, the purpose, the interests but also the limits and the risks of regulatory impact assessment. Professor Ogus' work spotlights the interest of impact assessment methods in the field of public policy. Such methods became one of the basic principles of good governance requirement and to some extent of new public management approach. To put it in a nutshell, government's intervention must not be longer assessed exclusively in terms of legal compliance in public resource consumption. The control shifts from the input consumption to the outcomes, in other words the global effects, of a given public policy. Impact assessment requirements belong to such logic of public action. A cost-benefit analysis must be performed before deciding to implement a public decision.

We can begin by giving a rundown of Professor Ogus' paper. Professor Ogus first sets the purpose and the history of the implementation of regulatory impact analysis. He underlines that

* CNRS Research Fellow, Research Group on Law, Economics and Management – University of Nice Sophia-Antipolis, OFCE / Sciences Po. Paris.

a such tool becomes an important dimension of the new public management especially to guarantee that government regulations are proportioned to their purposes and reach them efficiently, that is to say at the cheaper cost. With this in mind, each new legal rule has to be assessed through cost-benefit method in order to establish if its potential benefits outweigh or justify its costs. If impact assessment methods rely on cost benefit analysis, they also inherit its limits. We must keep in mind that agent behavior does not change compulsorily in the indented way. In addition, all change can have indirect effects on other markets. Other pitfalls are caused by the difficulties to valuate non-marketable resources or to choose between the different normative criteria that can be used. Professor Ogus also underlines the difficulties induced by risk and uncertainty in this kind of assessment. The issue of risk is one of the most interesting because it highlights the potential divergences between scientific risk assessment and social subjective perceptions. It could induce some disproportionate responses, which can go against general interest (or welfare maximization). Consequently a flawed risk perception could lead to a sub-optimal decision. It's the same process for uncertainty. An excessive level of precaution could lead to devote an excessive level of resources to the prevention of a very hypothetical risk at the expense of the coverage of more probable ones. It could finally induce a worse collective outcome than the one which could arise in the absence of any regulation. The last point analyzed by Professor Ogus relies on the trade-off between cost-benefit method and cost-effectiveness one. He points out the fact that the European Guidelines of 2009 recommend in some cases to complement the first with the second one.[1] Cost-effectiveness analysis can explain – eventually justify – some regulatory deci-

---

[1] European Commission, (2009), *Impact Assessment Guidelines*, SEC (2009)92.

sions, which make no sense in a narrow economic sense but are however rational in the political sense.[2]

Through these comments, we discuss of Professor Ogus' paper by putting the regulatory impact assessment in perspective with law and economics debates. There are some very close connections between the politico-economic analysis performed by Anthony Ogus and the economic analysis of law. In other words, many of the debates around the economic analysis of law make also sense for impact assessment methods. Such a connection between law and economics and regulatory impact assessment is hardly surprising. Indeed, Professor Ogus published in 1998 in the *European Journal of Law and Economics*[3] a striking paper about, the finally modest, contribution to law and economics to regulatory appraisal despite its purpose of predicting the impact of legal rules on behavior.

To that purpose we first analyze regulatory impact assessment in the framework of the three levels of law and economics analysis found by L. Kornhauser. As we spotlight, impact assessment has undoubtedly a close connection with the predictive and above all the normative one. This last one interestingly corresponds to the economic analysis of law in a Posnerian perspective. In order to go more into details on that point we investigate in our second part what the underlying hypothesis are. They are made, both in terms of determinants of human action and relatively to the capacity of the judge or the legislator to define socially desirable outcomes. In our third part, we successively discuss five points of convergence of the issues at stake in law and economics debates and in regulatory assessment ones. A first one deals with the objectives, which are ascribed to the legal rules. The other ones are relative to the difficulty to adopt such pre-

---

[2] Posner E., (2004), "Transfer Regulations and Cost-Effectiveness Analysis", *Duke Law Journal*, volume 53, pp.1067-1100.

[3] Ogus A., (1998), "Regulatory Appraisal: a Neglected Opportunity for Law and Economics", *European Journal of Law and Economics*, vol.6, pp.53-68.

dictive or even normative views. Then, we consider the possible
bias of such analysis, the issues induced by risk or uncertainty,
the limits of such constructivist conception of law, in terms of
judge or legislator capacity to design optimal rules, and finally
the difficulties caused by agent strategic responses to a shift in
legal rules. To draw a conclusion of this parallel between regulatory impact assessment, law and economics, we wonder about the
proper scopes of such methods.

I. IMPACT ASSESSMENT IN PERSPECTIVE WITH
THE THREE LEVELS OF LAW AND ECONOMICS

This logic is also closely linked to law and economics principles and more particularly to economic analysis of law recommendations. Following Lewis Kornhauser's taxonomy, it would
be possible to distinguish three different levels of analysis in law
and economics.[4]

The first one, and undoubtedly the original one, is a descrip-
tive purpose. When an economist considers law, it is mainly to
assess its economic consequences. As economic phenomena cannot be seen as purely driven by physical laws, it is impossible to
analyze them without considering them as social constructs. An
economic behavior cannot be comprehended in isolation from
social or legal frameworks. It was one of the main contributions of the German Historical School to underline the necessity to analyze economic phenomena as embedded within legal
and institutional environments. In other words economic agent
decisions and choices are shaped by legal institutions. Studying
economic process supposes to take into account this legal-eco-

---

[4] Kornhauser L., (1985), « L'analyse économique du droit », *Revue de Syn-
thèse*, série 3, n° 118-119, pp. 313-329.

nomic nexus as old institutionalism approach recommends. As the legal framework has a major impact on economic choices, one of the roles devoted to economics is to assess the consequences of a given change in legal rules or a new government policy.

A second analysis level is given by the predictive purpose of law of economics. As economic decisions are partially determined by legal rules, it is possible to assess to what extend such choices would be affected or modified by a change in law. So economics would have a second purpose. This one no longer plays ex post but from now ex ante. A preliminary assessment of the possible impact of a political decision in terms of social welfare could enlighten the policy makers as to the consequences of a given project. Such a role is not only conceivable for government policies; it is also possible to apply it to judicial decision. According to Oliver Holmes, in its seminal book *The Common Law*, written in 1881[5], the judge decides nor from the implementation to the case of a legal syllogism or a given economic or from a social theory, but according to its experience. Experience in such context could be as well interpreted as its understanding of social expectations about its own judgment or as its own expectations about the future consequences of its decision on the behavior of a bad man. As Holmes underlined, law is only for him what courts decide. So, judicial decisions have to be designed with taking into consideration their future impact on economic agent behaviors. As a government decision a judgment could be assessed in terms of collective impacts. The logic in Becarria's works during the eighteenth century or the theory of the optimal sanction from Gary Becker in 1968, are nothing but a few illustrations of such predictive purpose of economic analysis.[6]

---

[5] Holmes O.W., (1881), *The Common Law*

[6] Becker G., (1968), "Crime and Punishment: An Economic Approach", *Journal of Political Economy*, 76 (2), pp.813-846.

Such purpose leads us to the third level of law and economics, the normative one. As economic analysis is able to predict –with more or less reliability– the impact of a given decision, it could also help to define what would be a legal change which could allow obtaining a given result. Such an ambition is certainly the most difficult and controversial one. It also reflects a shift in economics from the law and economics approach to the economic analysis of law. The main purpose is no longer to assess the economic consequences of a given rule of a given policy but to design a legal rule to obtain a result, which is conceived as socially desirable.[7] For example, while R. Coase considers that the purpose of law and economics relies on the "study of the influence of the legal system on the working of the economic system",[8] Posner assigns to the economic analysis of law the role to perform an economic analysis of the working of the legal system.[9]

---

[7] For R. Posner, the purpose of the Common Law is to improve economic efficiency. As a consequence, we can consider that economic analysis is a powerful tool not only to assess the consequences of a given legal rule on economic efficiency but also to design legal rules, which would impact individual choices favorably in terms of social welfare.
For a discussion, see :
Posner R., (1979), "Some Uses and Abuses of Economics in Law", *University of Chicago Law Review*, vol. 46, 281, pp. 287-297.

[8] Coase R., (1996), "Law and Economics and W. Brian Simpson", *Journal of Legal Studies*, vol. 25, n°1, pp.103-119.

[9] Harnay S. and Marciano A., (2009), "Posner, Economics and the Law: From *Law and Economics* to an *Economic Analysis of Law*," *Journal of the History of Economic Thought*, vol. 31, n°2, pp. 215-232.

II. IMPACT ASSESSMENT AND NORMATIVE LAW AND ECONOMICS

This third purpose supposes to formulate some very involving hypothesis upon social phenomena and human action but also to decide about what decision criteria will be chosen. Before analyzing in broad terms, the assumptions of the normative law and economics, we must keep in mind the cautious approach developed by Professor Ogus in a paper published in 2004 in the *Chicago Kent Law Review*. Law and Economics could be useful to legal scholars on its own predictive level, "rather than its (perhaps overexposed) normative dimension".[10]

1. HOW TO DECIDE ECONOMIC AGENTS

First, we have to accept a model of human action in which people determine rationally their choices in order to maximize their well-being. Different conceptions of such notion could be adopted. One can consider that utility could be used for this matter; another could prefer to use monetary wealth as a proxy, in order to avoid some of the pitfalls of the first notion. But, whatever the choice, it is necessary to suppose that a given rule plays as a price, which is integrated in the rational agent's economic trade-off. To caricature, a legal rule can be analyzed as an economic stimulus. It changes the price of an activity. If we would consider that each individual decision is based on a cost-benefit analysis, it changes the parameters of agent market (and not market) decisions. So by a reverse engineering process we can deduce how a rule has to be modified in order to induce a desirable social shift.

---

[10] Ogus A., (2004), "What Legal Scholars can Learn from Law and Economics", *Chicago-Kent Law Review*, vol.79, pp.383-401.

This leads us to the second critical dimension: How can a collectively desirable result be defined? What are the possible criteria? The risk of incurring in over-simplification nnotwithstanding, we may propose that two alternative criteria are available. The first one is the well-known Pareto criterion. A shift is socially desirable if it induces an improvement in the welfare of one agent without damaging those of another. Such a requirement is excessively paralyzing. With few exceptions, a government decision always produces 'winners' and 'losers'. A response to such a deadlock is to use the Kaldor-Hicks criterion: A shift is desirable if the absolute value of gains of the 'winner' exceeds the losses of the others.

Ideally, the latter should be compensated. But we must keep in mind that such compensation could be merely hypothetical. Indeed, in some situations compensation is not feasible. For example, when the benefits are concentrated in few agents and the negative impacts spread over many people, mandating the 'winner' to compensate for the collective harm produced, this could be counterproductive in terms of aggregate social welfare, if only because of the induced transaction costs. In addition, in some cases even if compensation were to be possible, it would not be desirable. It could be, for example, the case of a law, which terminates exclusive legal rights. It could be seen as undesirable in terms of social justice or equity to impose a compensation for the former monopolist –we can even observe numerous examples of such requirements in economic history. One of the last –and certainly one of the least controversial– was the sunk cost compensation for former monopolists in the energy sector. As they decided to make investments within the framework of the former regulation, their expected cash flows were significantly impacted by the new rules of the game. It appears necessary to correct the effects of what could be seen as a contractual hold-up allowed by discretionary public choices. Consequently, a transitory regime was set to allow such firms to benefit from additional resources in order to meet their initial requirements in terms of financial returns.

III. THE UNDERLYING CONCEPTION OF LEGAL RULES

1. THE OBJECTIVES OF LEGAL RULES

More generally, impact assessment methods raise some concerns about the capacity of both the legislator and the judge to dispose from the whole knowledge necessary to take an optimal decision and about the range of economic advices.

Let us first consider the second point. What could really be the point of view of an economist about a public policy? Is it possible to encompass all the social dimensions of a given alternative? Does the economist have to consider the wealth distribution consequences of the decision? An economic approach to public decision-making –the same reasoning that could be applied to competition policies– should only consider economic efficiency, leaving aside all distributional concerns? For example, according to Richard Posner, judges –considered as interstitial legislators– have to concentrate their concerns on efficiency because they do not dispose of adequate tools and choice criteria to deal with other values as redistribution.[11] A striking example of such a question could be given with the Chicago-style approach to competition economics. In the middle of the last century,

---

[11] Posner R., (2003), *Economic Analysis of Law*, 6th edition.

both according the ordo-liberal approach in Europe and the Harvard "structuralist" School in the United States, competition policy has to pursue not only an objective of economic efficiency, but also an equitable one.[12] For the Chicago School, the only purpose of competition law is to ensure the maximization of the consumer welfare. Other purposes, such as the protection of small and medium sized firms or distributional dimensions, have to be realized through other public policies, for example, those concerning taxation. As R. Bork stated "Antitrust [...] has nothing to say about the ways prosperity is distributed or used. Those are matters for other laws. Consumer welfare as the term is used in antitrust has no sumptuary or ethical component. [...] It can only increase collective wealth by requiring that any lawful products [...] be produced and sold under conditions most favorable to consumers".[13]

2. TAKING INTO ACCOUNT POSSIBLE BIAS

One of the main reasons why impact assessment tends to privilege strictly economic dimensions relies on the fact that such evaluation methods overweigh the variables which are easily quantifiable. As a consequence, impact assessment procedures devote more importance to what could appear to be objective data than more qualitative dimensions, which could be seen as subjectively assessable. If we consider that impact assessment draws on new public management procedures, we can underline that one of its essential purposes is to promote the accountability of public management. Accountability can be considered improved

---

[12] Budzinski O., (2003), "Pluralism of Competition Policy Paradigms and the Call for Regulatory Diversity", *working paper*, n° 14/2003, Philipps Universität Marburg, 49p.

[13] Bork R.H., (1978), *The Antitrust Paradox – A Policy at War with Itself*, Free Press, New York.

if public management is more rule-driven than discretionary. Consequently, all qualitative dimensions would be under evaluation for the greater benefit of strictly economic, not to say monetary, reasons. One of the most representative examples of such bias is given by the preliminary assessment procedures used for public-private partnership contracts. The British public sector comparator, and the French preliminary assessor as well, tends to privilege the financial aspects of projects at the expense of other dimensions such as the quality of services delivered to final consumers or the contract's flexibility. As a consequence, there is a real risk to see financial data become the sole dimensions of the public contractor trade-off between a traditional procurement scheme (eventually an in-house service performance) and a public-private partnership. Such assessments present another common feature with impact assessment limits, as Antony Ogus' paper demonstrates. This common feature is the difficulty to deal with risk and uncertainty.

3. DEALING WITH RISK AND UNCERTAINTY

The limits of impact assessment methods when risk and uncertainty is at stake could also be illustrated with another example originating in competition policy. Initially, competition authorities are blamed for performing excessively form-based assessments of market practices –in cases concerning behaviours contrary to accepted competition standards– which rely only on legal dimensions. Chicago School economics applied to competition policy often criticize the consequences of such appraisals on the sole criterion of consumer welfare maximization. Let me give two different examples of such phenomena in competition law enforcement.

The first deals with merger and acquisition control, and the second with dominant firm unilateral practices in exclusionary abuse claims. A project of merger or acquisition has to be firstly notified to the appropriate competition authority. This authority must perform an assessment of the project, in other words, of its economic impact. In 'old-style' competition law enforcement, a project could be rejected as soon as it would be considered to create or reinforce a single-firm market dominance. According to Chicago economics, as applied to competition policy, such assessment could lead to the groundless refusal of a project, which, however could have increased consumer welfare. As a consequence, competition authorities moved to a more economic approach, in which a balance is reached between the detriment to competition (in terms of market dominance) and the gains made in efficiency, which would derive from the merger project. But, in practice, a frequent bias could arise. If damage to the competitive structure of the market is certain –or possibly by assessment according to the distribution of probability–, it also appears that the asserted efficiency gains are hypothetical. It is a common observation that mergers and acquisitions rarely produce the gains expected. In addition, in the context of imperfect and asymmetric information, the competition authority can expect that the firms will exaggerate such potential benefits. Consequently, when the damages to competition are taken into account, the potential benefits are under-assessed.

The same phenomenon can also be analysed for anticompetitive practices. A practice practiced by a dominant firm, which could lead to competitor exclusion, could avoid sanction on the condition that it would produce some gains in efficiency, which tend to out-weigh damages to fair competition. Such practices could be accepted if they do not lead to the complete elimination of competition, and, if it is necessary to realize such oversights, if these benefits exceed the infringements of free competition and if the final consumer benefits significantly from them. Again, when the free market damages seem certain, and the gains in efficiency remain hypothetical and subject to skepticism, they are finally mimimalised in the assessment performed by the competition authority.

4. QUESTIONING LEGISLATOR OR JUDGE CAPACITY TO DESIGN OPTIMAL LEGAL RULES

A second dimension in impact assessment which is questionable is relative to the capacity given to the judge or the legislator to ascertain from all the knowledge that necessary to take an optimal decision. It is the crucial point in the controversies between Hayekian and Posnerian perspectives relative to the ability of the judge to act as an interstitial legislator. Hayek stated that the legislator is not able to aggregate the whole of the information dispersed across market participants.His reasoning relies on the fact that he makes a distinction between scientific knowledge, in other words, data, which can possibly be aggregated and transferred to the decision makers, and market knowledge, which is idiosyncratic to a given economic agent and which is specific to the circumstances of time and place.[14] On the contrary, Posner assumes that the legislator –or the judge– is able to synthesise all the knowledge necessary to deliver an optimal ruling or to make an optimal decision in terms of wealth maximization.

In other words, Hayekian and Posnerian perspectives give contradictory insights about the nature of knowledge and the role of judges or legislators as producers of economically efficient rules. Posner, and the economic theory of legal logic, assume that legislators are capable of collecting large amounts of both factual and theoretical knowledge and, through economic logic, conscientiously develop and implement law according a given objective in terms of social outcomes. On the contrary, the neo-Austrian

---

[14] Hayek F., (1945), "The Use of Knowledge in Society", *American Economic Review*, vol.35, n° 4, September.

perspective tends to be more doubtful about the capacity of the legislator (even an interstitial one, such as a judge) to collect and weight all the knowledge necessary to develop conscientiously legal rules in order to achieve a given objective collectively defined. Positive and normative conceptions of law and economics lead to very irreconcilable views on impact assessment methods. If we consider law as either a spontaneous order or a constructed one, we cannot attribute to impact assessment the same virtues.[15]

For R. Posner, legal rules must be designed in order to help to realize cetain social goals, which mainly consist in economic efficiency, in so many words, wealth maximization. Consequently, judges "can, do and should" base their decisions on economic principles, as legislators must do, to improve the economic efficiency of the law. The link with impact assessment is obvious. Judges and legislators are supposed to forecast the future consequences of their decisions upon economic efficiency. They must arbitrate between different rules (alternative decisions) with economic efficiency as the criterion.[16]

The breaking point between Hayek and Posner is the possibility to anticipate how a legal rule is susceptible not only to influence behavior but also, in some extent, to determine it. For Hayek, a judge cannot be able to collect and synthesize the necessary data and to perform such economic balances or even to "predict whether the adoption of a particular rule will make society better or worse off".[17] In other words, the purpose of normative law and economics could appear in such perspective as a *fatal conceit*,[18] not only because the judges cannot dispose of all the necessary knowledge, but also because they cannot anticipate

[15] Zywicki T.J. and Sanders A.B., (2008), "Posner, Hayek and the Economic Analysis of Law", *Iowa Law Review*, vol.93, pp. 560-603.

[16] Posner R., (2003), *Economic Analysis of Law*, 6th edition.

[17] Zywicki T.J. and Sanders A.B., (2008), *op. cit.*

[18] The Judge could be seen as economic actor able to optimally allocate resource in the economy, as a central-planner theoretically does...

what will be the effective consequences of similar decisions. In other words, it is impossible to presume that an optimal designed rule (if such an ambition is even realistic) will produce an optimal (or even the expected) effect.[19] The point is that not only judges (or legislators) do not search for realizing a given policy objective through judgments or the producing of legal norms; it is in fact impossible to achieve such objectives by these means because it is impossible to consider that individual decisions will be mechanically and categorically modified by these kindsof stimulus in the anticipated sense and to the necessary extent.

5. DEALING WITH ECONOMIC AGENT OPPORTUNISTIC RESPONSES TO THE RULES

In the same way, even the impact assessment performed by the decision maker is optimal in economic terms, that is to say if qualitative dimensions are well assessed and risk and uncertainty correctly managed, there is no insurance that the rule will produce its expected effects. We can give some examples of such phenomena by considering both the microeconomic and the macroeconomic point of view.

A) A MICROECONOMIC POINT OF VIEW

Firstly, market participants do not mechanically reply to price stimuli, accepting that rules in our case are conceived as price signals, which are designed to modify agents' decisions in a collectively optimal fashion. Legal rules do not function in an algorithmic manner. Economic agents do not react mechanically to these signals. Economic behavior cannot be completely ex-

---

O'Driscoll G.P., (1980), "Justice, Efficiency, and the Economic Analysis of Law: A Comment on Fried", *Journal of Legal Studies*, vol.9, p.355.

[19] Hayek F., (1973), *Droit, Législation et Liberté*, Paris, PUF.

plained from the perspective of the stimulus of prices. There is a margen to allow for opportunistic or utilitarian adjustments or strategic opportunism of resources of action given by the rules.

A conventional example of such a phenomenon is certainly given by the analysis of I. Kirzner on profit maximization strategies developed from legal rules.[20] Every rule can produce profit opportunities, which could be strategically taken. Consequently, a rule cannot produce its expected effects. Its results would be sub-optimal, even if the rule were originally optimally designed. In other words, if a legal rule is imposed to curb market participant strategies, they would try to develop new self-beneficial systems or to adjust their strategies in order to evade its effects. If in some cases such adaptations might help correct the undesirable consequences of an unfortunate rule,[21] in other circumstances, they might also produce more undesirable effects.

In the same way, competition policy gives numerous examples of strategic uses of rules, not to say misuses. The case of nuisance suits is a good illustration of such phenomena. Filing a complaint makes sense for raising rival costs. It also allows unefficient firms to obtain in certain cases something like an "antitrust umbrella", in order to avoid exclusion from the market. It is, for example, the case of essential facility doctrines claims or some complaints concerning margin squeezes or exclusionary abuses. Finally, in other cases, strategic lawsuits can be used as tools to obtain settlements from competitors, which are detrimental to consumers.

---

[20] Kirzner I., (1978), « Government regulation and the market discovery process » in *Perils of regulation : a market process approach*, University of Miami, School of law, Coral Gables, FL, section IV, pp.13-19.

[21] Zywicki and Sanders took the example of the prohibition of some loyalty rebate schemes by the Robinson-Patman Act in the United States. Firms react by the issuance of coupons, which allows thwarting the negative effects of such prohibition, which was not coherent with consumer interests and by the way had adverse effects in terms of welfare maximization.
Zywicki T.J. and Sanders A.B., (2008), *op. cit.*

Another example of such processes could be found in product liability rules.[22] The well-known trade-off between negligence rules and strict-liability rules illustrates, according to the economic analysis of law, how the latter cannot bring out its expected effects because of the consequences on agents' incentives. For example, strict-liability rules are commonly accused, in literature, of encouraging morally hazardous phenomena (such as product misuse) whilst favouring parallel consumer pursuits.[23]

B) A MACROECONOMIC POINT OF VIEW

Secondly, impact assessment methods must integrate, to some extent, the limits caused in the foreseeable nature from the consequences of a given rule on human actions by rational expectations. Economic agents can perfectly anticipate the effects of a rule or a public decision. As a consequence, they can directly adapt their consequences to bring about the most beneficial results. The adjustments are optimal regarding the rules –if we suppose people want to maximize their interests (or more directly their wealth)– but certainly sub-optimal for the legislator. For example, if we consider the tipical case of the trade-off between unemployment and inflation described by the well-known Phillips Curve, we can see that a public policy, which tries to solve employment difficulties with a lax monetary policy, would have no effect in as much as people immediately and perfectly anticipate its impact on price levels. This same logic could be used to put Lucas' critic of macroeconomics into sights. A macroeconomic policy, which is designed based on agent behaviour modelling, will not produce its expected effects just because its immediate impact is to induce them to adapt their decisions according to these new rules of the game, such as considering it a perfectly rational and immediate

[22] Cooter R. and Ulen T., (1999), *Law and Economics*, 3rd edition, Addison-Wesley-Longman, Massachusetts.
[23] Zywicki T.J. and Sanders A.B., (2008), *op. cit.*

response from an economic agent to accept a rule modification that would possibly lead it to the deprevation of the greater part of its anticipated desirable effects.

IV. CONCLUSION

Finally, a last dimension that we must consider is related to the scope of the impact assessment, especially if we consider that these studies will over-evaluate economic dimensions in general and monetary ones in particular. Indirectly, it could lead us to reflect upon the scope of the economic analysis of law (and perhaps of economic science as a whole). Is impact assessment legitimate solely when market-oriented politics are concerned? Could it be applied to all dimensions of the law, considering that an economic approach is valid for all dimensions of human action as soon as it is determined to be a rational choice between mutually exclusive options and limited means?

In this sense, whilst impact assessment methods are applied to not only strictly economic concerns, it is necessary to adopt them to a larger acceptance relevant to the economic methods that give explanation to human actions. In other words, it supposes an economic tool to analyse the non-market dimensions of agent behaviours. It could persuade the use of methods to ascribe hypothetical prices to explain or to forecast agent choices. Two main difficulties should be emphasized. The first deals with the methods used to work out such prices. The second is linked to the capacity of economic forecasting methods used to predict non-market behaviour.

The first question deals with the method used for determining hypothetical prices. As an economic analysis of law, impact assessment methods have to rely on utility maximisation methods. In order to overcome the difficulties induced by utilitarian criteria (such as aggregation or comparison from one agent to another), R. Posner takes the choice of wealth maximisation. In the same way, impact assessment methods have to use monetary quantifications. The difficulties arise for non-market issues. Even if a market exists for certain goods (health, environment), it is not sure that the interests of the following generations are well taken into account by them. In such circumstances, when markets do not yet exist, how should we define how much we should be willing to pay?[24] In the same manner, it is necessary to determine implicit prices for domestic occupations or in other theoretical cases that put prices on hedonistic endeavours,with all the inherent difficulties of such exercises.

Impact assessment methods suppose – as economic analysis of law – that the world is predictable. As economic analysis of law only considers the market in terms of equilibrium, there are no coordination issues or questions relating to the development of knowledge, as in the Austrian perspective, which conceives the market as a process. Consequently, "the fundamental social problem therefore is how to arrange social, legal and economic institutions so as to maximize social wealth in equilibrium.[25]

Does economic analysis provide efficient tools to explain non-market decisions? A response could be Becker's definition of economics. For him, "the economic approach is clearly not restricted to material goods and wants, nor even to the market sector".[26] In other words, it is possible to develop an economic analysis of non-market choices. As soon as scare resources are

[24] The wealth in the Chicago sense does not seen to be limited to market prices. It also encompasses the consumer surplus which is assessed by the difference between consumer's disposition to pay and the market price. In the same way, global wealth includes the consumer surplus (e.g., its rofits from the transaction).

[25] Zywicki T.J. and Sanders A.B., (2008), *op. cit*

[26] Becker G.S., (1976), *The Economic Approach to Human Behavior*, The Chicago University Press, Chicago.

at stake, economics are able to explain and, meanwhile, forecast human decisions.[27] Consequently, economics could be used in impact assessment even when the rule does not directly concern market regulation.

These considerations certainly surpass the links between law and economics and its theoretical evolutions on the one hand, and impact assessment methods on the other. Nevertheless, if we consider the relation that the law and economics, and moreover, the economic analysis of the law are based on the fundamental proposition of the evaluation of legal norms within an economic process, and possibly on the need to design optimal norms to achieve a determined political objective(optimal in terms of the maximization of well-being), it would appear logical that the this logic is indivisibly joined to with the philosophy of impact assessment.

In this sense, the purpose of impact assessment methods could be summarized by the objective that R. Posner gave in the *Journal of Legal Study* in 1972, in response to the search for a theory of legal decision-making.[28] The ever-increasing involvement of the economist in the formulation of legal norms, through preliminary impact assessment, is a response to the recognition of the importance of such rules on economics process. As soon as economists no longer consider legal rules as a given, in order to consider them as objects of analysis, they can catch them as variables of the actions to improve economic efficiency.

---

[27] Economics "is the study of allocation of scarce means to satisfy competing ends".
Becker G.S., (1971), *Economic Theory*, Albert Knopf, New York.

[28] Posner R., (1972), "An Afterword", *Journal of Legal Studies*, volume 1, n°2, pp.437-440.

CHAPTER III

IMPACT ASSESSMENT AND COST-BENEFIT ANALYSIS: WHAT DO THEY IMPLY FOR POLICYMAKING AND LAW REFORM?

Susan Rose-Ackerman*

* Henry R. Luce Professor of Jurisprudence (Law and Political Science), Yale University. This article is based on a presentation at the Workshop on Regulatory Impact Assessments organized by Jean-Bernard Auby at Sciences Po, 24 November 2010. The discussion of cost-benefit analysis is drawn from Susan Rose-Ackerman, *Putting Cost-Benefit Analysis in Its Place: Rethinking Regulatory Review* U. MIAMI L. REV. (2011).

CONTENTS

CASE 1: CORRECTING MARKET FAILURES 106

CASE 2: OTHER VALUES IN REGULATORY POLICY 116

CASE 3: LARGE-SCALE MULTI-GENERATION PROBLEMS: IR-
    REVERSIBILITIES AND CATASTROPHES 117

CONCLUSION 121

I MPACT Analysis (IA) is now a legal mandate in France. But just what does that mean? Ultimately, the Constitutional Council may decide, but in the meantime politicians and policy analysts need to confront its promises and its ambiguities. IA is grounded in a commitment to promulgating policies that have positive net benefits while at the same time improving public accountability and incorporating other values.[1] In the European Union and at the OECD, a bandwagon in favor of IA may be starting that needs to be subject to critical scrutiny before it acquires the status of conventional wisdom.[2] I provide the beginnings of such a critique by connecting the institutionalization of IA in France to the debate over the proper role of cost-benefit analysis (CBA) in policymaking and regulatory reform in the United States.

---

[1] On impact assessment in European Union member states, see ANDREA RENDA, IMPACT ASSESSMENT IN THE EU (2006); Jonathan B. Wiener, *Better Regulation in Europe*, 59 CURRENT LEGAL PROBS. 447 (2006). For material on the European Union's impact-assessment initiative, consult *Impact Assessment–Key Documents*, EUR. COMMISSION, http://ec.europa.eu/governance/impact/key_docs/key_docs_en.htm (last updated Sept. 28, 2010).

[2] For arguments that cost-benefit analysis has already become and ought to continue to be a routine tool for policymaking, see RICHARD L. REVESZ & MICHAEL A. LIVERMORE, RETAKING RATIONALITY: HOW COST-BENEFIT ANALYSIS CAN BETTER PROTECT THE ENVIRONMENT AND OUR HEALTH (2008); CASS R. SUNSTEIN, THE COST-BENEFIT STATE: THE FUTURE OF REGULATORY PROTECTION (2002); John D. Graham, *Saving Lives Through Administrative Law and Economics*, 157 U. PA. L. REV. 395, 456–83 (2008) at 515–16. *But see* FRANK ACKERMAN & LISA HEINZERLING, PRICELESS: ON KNOWING THE PRICE OF EVERYTHING AND THE VALUE OF NOTHING (2004); SIDNEY A. SHAPIRO & ROBERT L. GLICKSMAN, RISK REGULATION AT RISK: RESTORING A PRAGMATIC APPROACH (2003). On the quality of government cost-benefit analysis see Robert W. Hahn & Patrick M. Dudley, *How Well Does the U.S. Government Do Benefit-Cost Analysis*, 1 REV. ENVTL. ECON. & POL'Y 192 (2007).

An amendment to the French Constitution in 23 July 2008 provides that an organic law must govern the presentation of bills tabled in the National Assembly or the Senate. "Where there is no such compliance, the bills cannot be included on the agenda. In the event of disagreement between the president of the chamber examining the bill and the prime minister about disregard for – or misunderstanding of – the rules concerned, the matter is referred to the Constitutional Council (Article 39). This vague requirement was codified in an Organic Law of 15 April 2009, which took effect in the fall of 2009.[3] It requires that whenever the government presents a bill to the legislature, it must submit an impact analysis (IA). The IA must be prepared prior to the review of the draft by the Council of State. It will then accompany the bill when it is sent to the legislature in a public document available to anyone who wishes to consult it, both inside and outside the legislature. The assembly has ten days to determine if the IA is adequate (Organic Law, article 9) and can, at its own discretion, decide if amendments from members of parliament should also be subject to an evaluation before they are discussed (Organic Law, article 15). The Law explains what an IA is supposed to contain. To quote from Article 8, the IA must specifically detail:

- the way the bill dovetails with European legislation in force or being prepared, and its impact on the domestic legal system;
- the status of application of the law at the national level in the area(s) covered by the bill;
- the conditions of application over time of the envisaged provisions; ...
- [the application to local authorities and overseas territories] ...;

---

[3] Loi Organique relative à l'application des articles 34-1, 39 et 44 el la Constitution, No 2009-403, article 8.

- the evaluation of the economic, financial, employment and environmental impact and the financial costs and benefits expected from the provisions envisaged for each category of public administration and natural and legal persons concerned, indicating the calculation method used;
- the evaluation of the consequences of the provisions on public-sector employment;
- the consultations carried out prior to the referral to the Council of State; and
- the provisional list of implementation legislation necessary.

To an American observer, this is a striking development, and it will be fascinating to determine if the IA requirement affects the French lawmaking process. In France, IA is still a relatively new and unfamiliar concept, yet in one leap the French state has committed itself to a massive application of the technique in the highly political area of statutory drafting. This contrasts sharply with the American case. Although any US administration would be wise to back up its proposals with data and arguments and although Congress has greater staff resources than most parliamentary legislatures, the process of submitting, discussing and approving statutes in the US is not governed by enforceable legal standards beyond the need for a bill to pass both houses by majority vote and to be signed by the president (or to be passed over his veto by a two-thirds vote in each house) before it become law.

Although the French Organic Law is nominally procedural, the requirements have substantive implications. The government must evaluate the economic, financial, employment and environmental impacts and calculate the financial costs and benefits. It must be transparent about its calculations, presumably so others can critique its methods. No longer is the Council of State the primary arbiter of legislative quality. It has a first mover advantage because it continues to review drafts before presentation to the legislature. However, the draft that is sent to the legislature can now be subject to more intelligent criticism both inside and outside the legislature on the basis of the IA and the data that the government supplies. Interest groups and concerned citizens have no legal right to challenge the quality of the analysis; only the legislative leaders can submit an IA analysis to the Constitutional Council for a judgment on its adequacy. This option ought to provide a limited check on the government, although the Constitutional Council may not be well equipped for a review task that requires economic and social science expertise.

In any case, it will be important to track the implementation of the Organic Law. Such a study is complicated, however, by substantial confusion about what it means to carry out an Impact Analysis. If these uncertainties are not confronted in a straightforward way, they could sink the entire enterprise as each new IA defines the term in a different way. The OECD, which has been a strong advocate of IA, is not of much help here. They simply list all the different goals of an IA without confronting the ways in which they might conflict in particular applications. Their spring 2010 report on progress in France is an extremely useful document that reviews and critiques the actions of the French state, but it neglects tensions at the heart of their advocacy of IA.[4]

Resolving these tensions is necessary, but I do not make a full scale effort to resolve them in this short essay. Rather, I outline the various aspects of IA; show how they may conflict, and then concentrate on the strengths and weaknesses of formal cost-benefit analysis, as a key inspiration for the move toward IA in Europe. My aim is to provide some balance to a discussion of CBA that is often carried out on both sides of the Atlantic in an excessively ideological fashion.

---

[4] OECD, Better Regulation in Europe: France (2010).

Fundamentally, Impact Analysis signals an interest in the functional efficacy of the law. The state should evaluate statutes and regulations to determine the effects they will have on human behavior and on the achievement of public benefits. That much seems uncontroversial. IA counsels a focus not on the formal properties of the law but on what it does. Neatness, clear drafting, and consistency are valuable only as means to an end, not as ends in themselves. Most descriptions of IA include provisions for transparency and public input prior to proposing new legal rules and also may contain requirements for ex post evaluation. But what criteria should one use to evaluate impacts? Here is where controversy arises.

One impetus for impact analysis, as for some types of cost-benefit analysis in the US, comes from portions of the business community interested in the reduction of red tape and regulatory burdens. A major theme of the OECD report on France is the claim that France has too many overlapping regulations and needs to simplify and rationalize the rules in a business friendly way.[5] The ranking in the World Bank's Doing Business reports are explicitly designed to give high marks to procedures that are cheap and fast with no concern for the broader social benefits of regulatory laws.[6] This is impact analysis as a reflection of libertarian philosophy that sees less as more with respect to state action. It may indeed be true that France has many legal rules that serve little purpose, but it is decidedly one-sided to presume that this is true. Hence, a more responsible position is to advocate cost-benefit analysis for both existing and proposed rules so that one can see if the benefits outweigh the costs. One should not assume that that the benefits are small just because the costs are burdensome.

---

[5] *Ibid.* Chapter 5, at 120-141 deals with the simplification of law.

[6] World Bank, 2011 Doing Business Report, available at http://www.doing-business.org/.

However, as soon as cost\benefit balancing is proposed, measurement issues loom large. How should one value health and life? How should the future be discounted? How should one value intangibles such as cultural and aesthetic values? Furthermore, how should the benefits and cost borne by different people and businesses be added up? Should one take account of the distribution of benefits and costs? The French statute requires the government to calculate benefits and cost "for each category of public administration and natural and legal persons concerned." But what does that mean? The statute does not require a formal cost\benefit analysis that seeks to maximize net benefits. Yet the use of the cost\benefit language suggests that something similar is envisaged. The Law, however, provides no guidance about how to proceed. Controversy over the proper role for cost\benefit analysis in public policymaking reveals deep tensions between economic and political values.

Three other themes also come up in the Organic Law and in discussions of "Better Regulation" by the OECD that point in different directions. First, documents discussing IA often refer to the value of public consultation, and the Law requires that government consultations be documented presumably both to encourage wide consultation and to guard against capture of the process by narrow interests.[7] Greater openness and participation of this sort accord with democratic values, but they may be in tension with technocratic, data-driven techniques if the participants are either poorly informed or a biased sample of the population or both. Second, IA is sometimes confused with the New Public Management, a technique for carrying out public programs that tries to import values from the private sector into state bureaucracy by introducing such practices as managing for results and incentive payments for civil servants as well as contracting out to

---

[7] Loi Organique, *supra* note 4, article 8; OECD *supra* note 5, chapter 3 at 68-85.

private firms.[8] Third, purely formal legal values are sometimes imported into IA, especially when traditional lawyers are charged with overseeing its implementation. The OECD document occasionally reflects this last set of values although, in practice, they may be in deep tension with the functional approach to law that is the fundamental principle of Impact Analysis.[9]

My aim in this essay is not to resolve these tensions but rather to help French legal scholars and practitioners understand the implications of embracing cost-benefit analysis as an aspect of Impact Analysis. True, the Organic Law only requires that costs and benefits be calculated and does not prescribe a particular method of aggregating the data. Nevertheless, once the monetary value of costs and benefits has been calculated, it may seem natural to locate the policy that maximizes net benefits. Thus, it is important for analysts and politicians to understand the implications of carrying out such an exercise. It implies a particular underlying normative commitment that is often defensible but that in other contexts may clash with important public values. IA has the benefit of pushing legal thinking beyond a concern with the purely formal nature of law. As a result, it opens a debate in public law over how to judge the quality of statutes and executive rules. The cost-benefit test of maximizing net benefits is one such criterion, but it is not the only one even in situations where data on costs and benefits can be calculated with confidence.

In the United States cost-benefit analyses are routinely performed for all sorts of policy initiatives. An Executive Order requires them for "major" rules issued by core executive branch agencies and expected to have at least $100 million per year impact on the economy. The Office of Information and Regulatory Affairs (OIRA) in the Executive Office of the President reviews

---

[8] Loi Organique, *supra* note 4, article 8; OECD *supra* note 5, chapter 5 where the work of the Director General for State Modernization (DHME) is described.

[9] OECD, *supra* note 5, chapter 5, at 120-141.

these reports and consults with regulatory officials on ways to improve the analysis and to make policy that reflects these principles, consistent with statute.[10] Although the director of OIRA must obtain Senate confirmation, the cost-benefit mandate itself is only embodied in an executive order that could be unilaterally rescinded or amended at any time by the president. Furthermore, the Executive Order only requires a study. It cannot require a government office to promulgate a rule that maximizes net benefits if that would be inconsistent with its statutory mandate, as it often is. The EO does not apply to spending programs, unless they are administered using rules, and rules issued by independent regulatory agencies such as the Federal Communications Commission or the Securities and Exchange Commission, are exempt. Unlike the current situation in France, draft statutes submitted by the executive to Congress need not include an impact analysis. Thus, CBA is institutionalized in the US, at least for major rules, but, beyond a few regulatory statutes, it has no formal legal standing.

---

[10] *See* Exec. Order No. 12,866 §§ 3(d)–(e), 3(f)(1), 6(a)(3)(C), 3 C.F.R. 638, 641, 645–46 (1993), *reprinted as amended in* 5 U.S.C. § 601 (2006). These sections of the executive order require agencies to prepare a cost-benefit analysis for all proposed and final rules that will have "an annual effect on the economy of $100 million or more or adversely affect in a material way the economy, a sector of the economy, productivity, competition, jobs, the environment, public health or safety, or State, local, or tribal governments or communities." *Id.* § 3(f)(1). To track current OIRA activities, see *Office of Information and Regulatory Affairs*, WHITEHOUSE.GOV, http://www.whitehouse.gov/omb/inforeg_default (last visited Oct. 7, 2010). The executive order does not apply to independent agencies, such as the Federal Trade Commission or the Federal Communications Commission, but many of them have also created policy analysis offices to review regulations and other policies. *See also* THOMAS O. MCGARITY, REINVENTING RATIONALITY: THE ROLE OF REGULATORY ANALYSIS IN THE FEDERAL BUREAUCRACY 18 (1991); Steven Croley, *White House Review of Agency Rulemaking: An Empirical Investigation*, 70 U. CHI. L. REV. 821, 824–30 (2003); Sidney A. Shapiro & Christopher H. Schroeder, *Beyond Cost-Benefit Analysis: A Pragmatic Reorientation*, 32 HARV. ENVTL. L. REV. 433, 446–47 (2008); Graham, *supra* note 3 at 456–83.

When is CBA an appropriate tool for policy evaluation? In the remainder of this essay I argue that CBA is a valuable technique for policymakers in the US and in France and the EU, but that a number of pressing current problems do not fit well into the CBA paradigm. In particular, climate change, nuclear accident risks, and the preservation of biodiversity can have very long-run impacts that may produce catastrophic and irreversible effects. CBA is suitable for many conventional policy issues that have limited but significant effects on society in the short to medium run. The best analogy is to the decisions made by large corporations when they decide how to invest to maximize profits over time. In such cases, both public agencies and firms seek to maximize the expected value of net gains, holding conditions in the rest of the world constant.[11] However, that is not an appropriate analogy for policies with a significant global impact. Hence the practice of IA in France should not import CBA wholesale for all draft statutes; the underlying nature of the policy problem should govern whether it is an appropriate technique.

I argue for a limited role for CBA on two grounds. First, cost-benefit analysis should be used to evaluate a limited class of policies, and even then it should be supplemented with value choices not dictated by welfare economics. Second, CBA presents an impoverished normative framework for policy choices that do not fall into this first category. In those cases, policy ought to be made on other grounds even though consideration of the costs and the benefits of a program is obviously a requirement for sound policymaking.

I do not wish to be misunderstood. I am not arguing for a return to a narrow, formal view of law. I favor technocratic analy-

---

[11] For a classic introduction to cost-benefit analysis, see E.J. MISHAN, COST-BENEFIT ANALYSIS (new & expanded ed. 1976); E.J. MISHAN & EUSTON QUAH, COST-BENEFIT ANALYSIS (5th ed. 2007) (1976). For a widely used text in policy schools that presents the basics, see DAVID L. WEIMER & AIDAN R. VINING, POLICY ANALYSIS (5th ed. 2011).

sis, such as that required by the Organic Law, that measures both costs and benefits in the most accurate way possible and that uses these data to make intelligent policy choices.[12] Problems arise, however, when the search for a single "best" policy forces analysts to make controversial assumptions simply to produce an answer that "maximizes" social welfare. The debate often conflates two related problems. First, analysts must resolve a set of difficult conceptual issues even where CBA is an appropriate technique on normative grounds. More fundamentally, the second set of problems strikes at the heart of the technique and makes it an inappropriate metric for the analysis of some policy issues.

First, difficult issues arise even if net-benefit maximization is a plausible public goal. In the best case for cost-benefit analysis, the program seeks to correct a failure in private markets, and the law's distributive consequences are not a major concern. Overall, distributive effects may be small or, if large, tilt in an egalitarian direction, as when a regulation limits the monopoly power of large businesses. Here, the main problems are measurement difficulties that are sometimes so fundamental that better analysis or consultation with experts cannot solve them. I am thinking mainly of debates over the proper discount rate for future benefits and costs; efforts to incorporate attitudes toward risk; and the vexing problems of measuring the value of human life, of aesthetic and cultural benefits, and of harm to the natural world. Disputes over these issues turn on deep philosophical questions—for example, valuing future generations versus balancing capital and labor in the production of goods and services; acknowledging the value of extra years of life versus "life" itself;

---

[12] See, for example, my advocacy of cost-benefit analysis as a background norm for courts to apply to the review of regulations designed to correct a market failure in SUSAN ROSE-ACKERMAN, RETHINKING THE PROGRESSIVE AGENDA: THE REFORM OF THE AMERICAN REGULATORY STATE (1992). Sunstein claims that, in a weaker and modified form, this is already what the courts do. SUNSTEIN, *supra* note 3, at 31–89.

taking risk preferences into account; and giving culture, ecosystems, and natural objects a place in the calculus. These issues do not have "right" answers within economics. They should not be obscured by efforts to put them under the rubric of a CBA. Politically responsible officials should resolve them in a transparent way.

Sometimes one policy is much better than many others under a wide range of assumptions. Sensitivity tests can explore this possibility. There is no need to resolve difficult conceptual and philosophical issues if the preferred outcome does not depend on the choice of a discount rate or the value given to human life. Such tests should be a routine part of the analytic toolkit and of the options presented to the ultimate policymakers.

Second, many policies raise important issues of distributive justice, individual rights, and fairness, especially between generations. Talk of "net-benefit maximization" does not help illuminate these value choices. These issues raise measurement problems, but the difficulties with CBA run deeper. Even if everything could be measured precisely, CBA would be an inappropriate metric. Attempts to add distributive weights to CBA are fundamentally misguided. They suppose that technocrats, especially economists, can resolve distributive justice questions.[13] The distributive consequences of policies should be part of the public debate over policies, aided by technocrats who can help to outline the distributive consequences of various policies. The main analytic problem is familiar to students of tax incidence.

---

[13] For a recent attempt to revive the concept of a social-welfare function (SWF) weighted toward those with low levels of utility, see Matthew D. Adler, *Future Generations: A Prioritarian View*, 77 GEO. WASH. L. REV. 1478 (2009) [hereinafter Adler, *Future Generations*]; *see also* Matthew D. Adler, *Risk Equity: A New Proposal*, 32 HARV. ENVTL. L. REV. 1 (2008) [hereinafter Adler, *Risk Equity*]. Adler, however, does not explain how a SWF ought to be constructed except that it should be strictly increasing and concave in utilities, and he argues that the resulting SWF, however derived, ought to be only an input into the process of policy choice.

The nominal cost bearer may pass on some of the costs to others. Distributive impacts are often difficult to measure and trace.

This second category includes policy issues that have a large impact on society at present and over multiple generations. Choices taken today may be irreversible or very costly to change, and they may risk large negative consequences for future generations. In these cases, the marginal, microanalytic framework characteristic of cost-benefit analysis is not appropriate even if one stays within a utilitarian framework. The problems—climate change, risks from the storage of nuclear waste, loss of biodiversity, to give a few examples—may have large pervasive impacts that stretch far into the future. Catastrophes are possible, even if not likely. These issues raise broad economic and social issues that require a different normative framework.

I begin with situations where cost-benefit criteria seem unproblematic—at least to those with some training in public-finance economics—that is, government efforts to correct market failures caused by such factors as externalities or monopoly power. Next, I expand my compass to include programs with other goals besides economic efficiency where the regulatory agency may seek cost-efficient solutions but cannot reduce a program's goals to an exercise in net-benefit maximization. Finally, based on these critiques I conclude with proposals for the restrained use of cost-benefit criteria and policy analytic techniques.

CASE 1: CORRECTING MARKET FAILURES

Markets are not always efficient. So much is the conventional wisdom in economics. Externalities, such as air and water pollution, impose costs that a profit-maximizing firm will not take into account unless regulatory laws or the threat of legal liability induce it to do so. Firms may seek to exercise monopoly power, and high entry barriers can make competition unlikely. Information about risks and harms may be unavailable or poorly processed by busy people who lack expertise. One can plausibly view regulatory laws that seek to correct such market failures through the lens of economic efficiency. They aim to correct problems in particular markets and sectors and are not appropriate loci for broad distributive justice concerns that implicate the overall distribution of income, wealth, and economic opportunity. True, some policies may have a particularly severe impact on a narrowly focused group, but such problems can be dealt with as a side constraint. Cost-benefit analysis was first applied to public infrastructure projects in the United States, and these remain good candidates for CBA to the extent that they too are filling a gap left by the private market and are expected to improve the efficient operation of the society.

For such policies, the goal of finding the most economically efficient solution seems relatively unproblematic. The problem is one of measurement, not principle. Yet, even here issues of principle arise in seeking appropriate measuring rods. At the most basic level, the goal is to maximize the net benefits from a policy, but how should one measure benefits and costs so that they are calculated in units that permit comparison? Jeremy Bentham, the ultimate source of the cost-benefit test, thought that individual utility could be measured in cardinal, interpersonal units and added up to get "the greatest happiness of the greatest number."[14] Suppose that marginal benefits fall as the scale of the policy increases and that marginal costs rise. Then welfare is at a maximum where the marginal benefits of the policy equal the marginal costs. Leaving aside debates over the implications of his principle for population policy, the key problem with Bentham's formulation is that no one knows how to measure utility so as to

---

[14] Jeremy Bentham, An Introduction to the Principles of Morals and Legislation 5 n.1 (photo. reprint 1907) (1823).

permit cardinal, interpersonal comparisons. Utility is not an essence that can be measured in units like inches and pounds and compared across people.[15] Fortunately, the Marginalist Revolution in economics at the end of the nineteenth century demonstrated that one could obtain the key results in economic theory by doing away with cardinal, interpersonally comparable utility and assuming only that people could order the options available to them in a consistent way. Eventually, revealed-preference theory showed how consistent preference relations could be derived from the study of the actual choices that individuals make in the market.[16] However, that revolution, elegant and important as it was, essentially did away with the normative analysis of policy in utilitarian terms. How could one tell if one policy was better than another if one could not compare the benefits and costs obtained by different people on a single metric? Pareto efficiency seemed to be all that was left—that is, a collection of possible outcomes where no one can be made better off without someone else being made worse off. All societies have many such points where no resources are being wasted but that differ in the way resources are allocated across individuals. One can identify market failures that put society below the efficiency frontier, but that leaves open a range of possible ways to move to an efficient outcome that might impose costs on some and benefits on others.

Many Pareto optimal results are not Pareto superior to the status quo; in other words, they are efficient, but getting there imposes costs on some and benefits on others. However, limiting policy only to Pareto superior options places a huge normative

---

[15] Van Neumann and Morgenstern developed a way to produce a cardinal utility scale for individuals based on their revealed preferences over lotteries, but it does not permit interpersonal comparisons. *See* John von Neumann & Oskar Morgenstern, Theory of Games and Economic Behavior (3d ed. 1953). For criticisms of this approach, see Ken Binmore, Rational Decisions 58–59 (2009).

[16] *See* Paul Anthony Samuelson, Foundations of Economic Analysis 90–124 (1948).

weight on the status quo distribution of resources. One would have to argue that the status quo is so fair and just that no one should be made worse off in order to provide social benefits for society.

Economists filled the breach in the mid-twentieth century by positing a "social- welfare function" to represent the way society somehow had decided to trade off the welfare of its citizens. Policymakers should maximize this function subject to the Pareto efficiency frontier to produce the best possible choice given limited resources—an outcome called, oddly, "the bliss point" by some economic analysts.[17] Kenneth Arrow's Impossibility Theorem demonstrated that such a function did not exist under minimal conditions, something that political scientists and practical politicians with experience of the clash of private interests may not have found surprising.[18] The economics profession seemed to be back to the mere claim that government policy could be used to correct market failures, but with little to say about which option was best.[19]

Cost-benefit analysis entered to fill the gap—first, for dam building by the Army Corps of Engineers and then for a broader range of policies, now including regulatory policies.[20] The basic

---

[17] *See id.* at 219–28; Abram Bergson, *A Reformation of Certain Aspects of Welfare Economics*, 52 Q.J. Econ. 310 (1938).

[18] *See* Kenneth J. Arrow, Social Choice and Individual Values (1951).

[19] A recent attempt to revive the concept by Matthew Adler has not solved the problem of making interpersonal comparisons in a persuasive way. *See* Adler, *Future Generations, supra* note 14; Adler, *Risk Equity, supra* note 14.

[20] On the early history of CBA in the federal government, see generally Public Expenditures and Policy Analysis (Robert H. Haveman & Julius Margolis eds., 1970) (assessing the state of policy analysis as a technique and as used within the federal government under the so-called, planning programming budgeting system). For an early collection of cost-benefit studies, see Measuring Benefits of Government Investments (Robert Dorfman ed., 1965). The first mention of cost/benefit balancing was in the 1936 Flood Control Act (P. L. 74-738) that required that "the benefits to whomever they accrue exceed the costs."

idea was to stick to a Benthamite utilitarian calculus but to use dollars or euros as the common metric instead of utilities. But there is a familiar problem with money. It does not have a one-to-one relationship to utility or happiness. A wealthy person may be willing to pay more for a benefit or to avoid a cost than a poorer person simply because he or she has more money to spend. However, if the program is small relative to the overall size of the economy and is not particularly skewed toward or away from one or another income group, market prices provide a reasonable proxy for the opportunity cost of resources used to carry out the policy. One can think of the policy as a marginal change toward the Pareto frontier with any serious distributive consequences highlighted and dealt with separately.[21]

Suppose one has allayed those fears and is ready to carry out a CBA that isolates the opportunity costs of a program and quantifies the benefits. In other words, the goal is to go beyond the budgetary costs to the government to ask if there are other social costs and to calculate the social benefits. The first task is the unproblematic one of itemizing benefits and costs measured in whatever units are available, be they dollars; expected lives saved or lost; health effects; or benefits to nature and to cultural or historical artifacts. These benefits and costs need to be quantified on an annual basis into the future with any uncertainties noted. These are the basic building blocks, and it is hard to criticize efforts to amass such information, except to note that scarce time and money may limit the quality and quantity of these data.

The easiest cases are those where a reasonably competitive market exists so that analysts can use market prices to measure opportunity costs on the assumption that the policy itself does not affect market prices. For example, when the US Army Corps of Engineers considers whether to build a dam, it can use the market prices of cement, sand, and labor to estimate costs. Farm-

---

[21] *See* MISHAN & QUAH, *supra* note 12; WEIMER & VINING, *supra* note 12.

ers benefit from cheaper irrigation water. This can translate into higher yields with the benefits measured by the increased sales of farm products, assuming the project has no impact on the overall market. The Corps can discount the stream of benefits back to the present using a discount rate that reflects the opportunity cost of capital. One can criticize the narrow focus on farm productivity and tangible costs, but given this view of the relevant costs and benefits, the Corps can rely on the larger market system to determine the opportunity costs and the benefits of the project.

Note how easily measurement problems arise in regulatory areas that do not track the simple case outlined above. Market prices are not available for many regulatory benefits and costs, and clever attempts to mimic the market are fraught with uncertainty. One possible discount rate is the opportunity cost of capital, but others argue for the consumers' rate of time preference—rates that, in our imperfect world, need not be equivalent. Using the opportunity cost of capital assures a capital-labor ratio for government programs in line with private investment incentives so that capital is not over- or underused by the government. A familiar problem in the Soviet Union was the overly capital-intensive nature of investment projects because capital, in Marxist theory, had no value and hence was overused. Using the rate of time preference requires one to know how citizens trade off present and future benefits and costs. If capital markets have imperfections, these rates need not be equal.[22]

If the benefits of correcting a market failure extend far into the future, the policy must incorporate the preferences of future generations. The logic of discounting means that these preferences are given little weight beyond fifty or so years at any discount rate close to the long-run rate of return on capital. For most conventional regulatory and spending programs this does not raise any particular problems. The policies correct market failures that will benefit people in the relatively short run, and most importantly, there are no irreversibilities. The effects do not threaten future generations with catastrophe or the possibility of bad macroeconomic outcomes. In general, one can presume that policies that make the economy more efficient and less subject to negative externalities will, on balance, be policies that future generations will want to continue. However, future generations can decide whether or not to pursue the policy. One still needs to set a discount rate or, at least, to perform a sensitivity analysis using a range of plausible rates, but the problem arises from market imperfections, not deep philosophical controversies. A key condition is that the policy is reversible in the future if the polity so decides. Present-day policymakers are not locking in future governments and are not subjecting future generations to irreversible catastrophic risks.

---

[22] For different perspectives articulated in articles collected in a *University of Chicago Law Review* symposium on intergenerational equity and discounting, see Geoffrey Heal, *Discounting: A Review of Basic Economics*, 74 U. CHI. L. REV. 59 (2007); Louis Kaplow, *Discounting Dollars, Discounting Lives: Intergenerational Distributive Justice and Efficiency*, 74 U. CHI. L. REV. 79 (2007); Douglas A. Kysar, *Discounting . . . on Stilts*, 74 U. CHI. L. REV. 119 (2007); Dexter Samida & David A. Weisbach, *Paretian Intergenerational Discounting*, 74 U. CHI. L. REV. 145 (2007); Cass R. Sunstein & Arden Rowell, *On Discounting Regulatory Benefits: Risk, Money, and Intergenerational Equity*, 74 U. CHI. L. REV. 171 (2007); W. Kip Viscusi, *Rational Discounting for Regulatory Analysis*, 74 U. CHI. L. REV. 209 (2007).

A second measurement issue is the treatment of risk. Many policies, especially in the area of health and safety, have uncertain benefits. They reduce the risk of cancer or lung disease, say, but there is a large margin of error in the estimates. Furthermore, even if the actual number of cases is known with a high level of certainty, no one may know ex ante who will actually get sick. These two kinds of risk raise different, but linked, issues of measurement.

The easiest case is one where the risk is distributed broadly and equally across the population, and the regulation reduces everyone's risk by an equal amount. Then the expected benefit would be the fall in risk multiplied by the average level of harm. If the harm is measurable, the only problem here is the possibility that people have different attitudes toward risk. Should one use expected values, which assume risk neutrality, or assume that people are generally risk averse? This is an issue either of predicting preferences or of arguing that government policy ought to adopt a particular attitude toward risk independent of the expected views of citizens.

More difficult cases arise when the science does not provide good estimates of the risk avoided by the policy. Then the risk is not limited to the identity of the victims but includes uncertainty about the actual level of harm avoided.[23] How precautionary should the regulation be when there is some chance that the harm avoided may be quite small? Should this depend upon estimates of risk aversion or, alternatively, on potential victims' fear of being harmed?

---

[23] See, for example, the debate over the Environmental Protection Agency's regulation of arsenic in drinking water. *See* ACKERMAN & HEINZERLING, *supra* note 3, at 91–98, 111–14; Jason K. Burnett & Robert W. Hahn, *A Costly Benefit: Economic Analysis Does Not Support EPA's New Arsenic Rule*, REG., Fall 2001, at 44; Lisa Heinzerling, *Markets for Arsenic*, 90 GEO. L.J. 2311 (2002); Cass R. Sunstein, *The Arithmetic of Arsenic*, 90 GEO. L.J. 2255 (2002); Richard Wilson, *Underestimating Arsenic's Risk: The Latest Science Supports Tighter Standards*, REG., Fall 2001, at 50.

Paradoxically, a policy may be harder to put in place if the state knows the identities of the victims, some of whom can be saved depending upon the stringency of the policy. Here, most receive no benefits, and a few receive very large benefits in extra years of life or enhanced quality of life. There is no reason to think that people value life and health in a linear fashion. Perhaps you will pay a small amount to improve the safety of your automobile so that the risk of a fatal car crash is reduced from, say, two percent to one percent, but one cannot multiply that number by 100 to determine the amount you must be paid to be killed for sure. Presumably, the curves relating willingness to pay and probability of death or serious injury are not linear. This poses the familiar conundrum in public policymaking where society spends large amounts to rescue particular individuals trapped in coal mines or under earthquake rubble but does not spend much up front to prevent such accidents in the first place.

Finally, beyond attempts to measure the value of life and morbidity, the market does not price other benefits and costs. These include the value of natural objects, and of historical and cultural monuments and practices. Travel-time studies can proxy recreation benefits so long as there is some parallelism between more distant sites and newly available ones closer to population centers. Property-value gradients can approximate the value of clean air. Surveys help place a value on saving wildlife. All of these methods have weaknesses, but, at least, they recognize that such benefits are not zero.[24] However, they often represent efforts to shoehorn impressionistic, subjective benefits into objective categories so that one is not sure what has been gained as

---

[24] For examples, see MARION CLAWSON & JACK L. KNETSCH, ECONOMICS OF OUTDOOR RECREATION (1966) (discussing travel costs); Peter A. Diamond & Jerry A. Hausman, *Contingent Valuation: Is Some Number Better Than No Number?*, 8 J. ECON. PERSP., Autumn 1994, at 45 (discussing contingent valuation); V. Kerry Smith & Ju-Chin Huang, *Can Markets Value Air Quality? A Meta-Analysis of Hedonic Property Value Models*, 103 J. POL. ECON. 209 (1995) (discussing property values).

a result of the Herculean assumptions needed to represent the benefits in dollar terms. Jonathan Wiener makes a distinction between "cold" and "warm" analysis. The former only includes benefits and costs that can be quantified in unproblematic dollar terms. The latter attempts to include the kind of benefits and cost outlined here. Wiener rejects "cold" CBA, but that seems an easy choice.[25] Even to the most committed cost-benefit proponent, "cold" analysis is simply incompetent analysis that does not satisfy the requirements of the technique. The only important conceptual issue raised by these difficult-to-measure factors is not the lack of good-dollar estimates, but the question of whether one should include any benefits and costs outside of those experienced by humans.

Thus, even when one can justify CBA as a normative matter, cost-benefit analysis faces at least four challenges. These are the problematic link between dollar totals and overall utility or net benefits; the choice of a discount rate; the treatment of risk and uncertainty; and the quantification of life, health, and other nonmarket values in the metric of dollars. Economic experts can highlight the wrong way to deal with these difficult problems, but they cannot ultimately solve these problems within the paradigm of welfare economics. Nevertheless, if analysts admit to these difficulties and carry out sensitivity analyses to see if the choice of discount rate or the use of proxies for nonmarket values matters to the outcome, a cost-benefit framework can help structure the policy debate. It can highlight the areas where judgments from outside welfare economics need to be brought in to make the final decision.

---

[25] *See* Wiener, *supra* note 2, at 483–89.

CASE 2: OTHER VALUES IN REGULATORY POLICY

Many regulations are meant to take account of values over and above economic efficiency. They guide transfer programs, such as Social Security, disability, or welfare. They are part of the administration of subsidy programs, such as those under the jurisdiction of the US Department of Agriculture (USDA). They are concerned with the fairness and equity of markets, such as the regulations of the US Equal Employment Opportunity Commission (EEOC) and some rules issued by the US Department of Labor and the Securities and Exchange Commission. They take on moral issues, as in the US Federal Communications Commission's (FCC) regulation of speech in the media.[26] A pure cost-benefit test, with its omission of distributive, fairness, and procedural concerns, would not encompass the purposes of these statutory mandates. Transfers from taxpayers to beneficiaries cancel out in a CBA. However, economic analysis can help locate cost-efficient options and can encourage agencies to find ways to give incentives to regulated firms to take these other values into account. It can complement traditional public administration reforms by introducing economic incentives into bureaucratic performance. But for such programs, CBA cannot be the criterion for the choice of a regulatory policy or the scale of a policy already mandated by statute.

One can frame the issue in terms of benefits and costs that should or should not enter the policy calculation. A strong utilitarian in the Benthamite tradition would not omit any gains or

---

[26] See, for example the recent controversy over the FCC's regulation over "fleeting expletives" which has already gone once to the U.S. Supreme Court on administrative law grounds and may return under a constitutional free-speech challenge. *See* FCC v. Fox Television Stations, Inc., 129 S. Ct. 1800 (2009), *rev'g* 489 F.3d 444 (2d Cir. 2007). On remand, the Second Circuit granted Fox's petition for review of the FCC's order. Fox Television Stations, Inc., v. FCC, 613 F.3d 317 (2d Cir. 2010).

losses, including those experienced by other sentient beings that feel pain. However, just as some want to include a wide range of weakly quantified benefits and costs, others argue for the exclusion of benefits and costs experienced by people as a result of their violent behavior or fraudulent activities. One possible guide is the criminal law. One can argue that if the state designates an action as a crime, then the gains to the perpetrator should not count in the social calculation.[27] In a similar vein, Matthew Adler and Eric Posner, in their effort to give CBA a new and distinctive grounding, argue for "laundering preferences" so only idealized ones count in the cost-benefit calculus.[28] They emphasize cognitive errors and biases in individual choices. However, an alternative based on actual political choices would use the criminal law as a measure of society's willingness to include certain benefits in the welfare calculus. One response in such cases is to require cost-effectiveness analysis and to help agencies design innovative programs that build on individual incentives to further program goals.

CASE 3: LARGE-SCALE MULTI-GENERATION PROBLEMS: IRREVERSIBILITIES AND CATASTROPHES

Welfare economists often study long-run macroeconomic policies where nothing is held constant. The normative framework has traditionally aimed to maximize the sustainable rate of economic growth, a policy position that obviously calls for the present generation to give up consumption in the interest of that

---

[27] Consistent application of this criterion, of course, might lead one to advocate decriminalization of some offenses.

[28] *See* MATTHEW D. ADLER & ERIC A. POSNER, NEW FOUNDATIONS OF COST-BENEFIT ANALYSIS (2006) at 36–38, 124–53.

goal.[29] Others have pointed out that there is no sound philosophical reason to favor the future over the present so that the goal should be to maximize the steady-state level of per capita income over time.[30] These models assume an infinitely lived civilization that can save and invest at different rates over time. If we add in the possibility that the present can impose large, irreversible and possibly catastrophic costs on the distant future, this raises the question of intergenerational obligation with particular salience.

To see the problem, consider the issue of climate change. Society will experience many of the benefits of climate change policy far in the future. Using even a low-end discount rate, say 5%, implies that a $1 benefit obtained 50 years in the future has a present value of 9 cents. At 3%, the present value is 23 cents and at 6% it is 5 cents. Suppose, to keep things simple, that all the benefits will accrue in year 50 and that they will be $5 billion. At 5%, the discounted present value of these benefits is $450,000, but it could be much higher or lower depending upon the discount rate chosen. Should that choice determine the global policy on climate change?

---

[29] *See, e.g.*, Edmund Phelps, *The Golden Rule of Accumulation: A Fable for Growthmen*, 51 AM. ECON. R. 638 (1961); *see also* Heal, *supra* note 23, at 67 (distinguishing, as I do, between small projects and those with economy-wide implications). For small projects, the consumers' rate of time preference or the return on capital is appropriate, as argued above. For projects with economy-wide implications, Heal argues that the pure rate of time preference should be used to discount utility, a rate that does not depend on the historical return to capital. His analysis draws on research on economic growth and assumes a utilitarian social-welfare function—not an obvious choice outside of economics. He does not explicitly consider irreversibilities, such as those that may arise with global warming. Both Heal and Kysar argue that for long-term policies, the discount rate is not exogenous but is a function of policy choices. *See* Kysar, *supra* note 23, at 128. Once again the distinction between partial and general equilibrium analysis is important. *But see* Viscusi, *supra* note 25 (arguing that no distinction should be made).

[30] *See, e.g.*, Samida & Weisbach, *supra* note 23.

Even those who advocate the equal worth of all generations accept a long-run positive growth rate as a fact of human history, in spite of the doubt cast on this claim as a result of climate change or other systemic risks. In other words, they assume that the market will generate a positive interest rate. That assumption produces much of the agonizing over the social rate of discount. Some claim that the lives of those in future generations should count equally to present lives and that that implies a zero discount rate for saved lives or sacrifices under some policy.[31] With a positive rate of return on capital, however, such a philosophical commitment to equity would imply that, under a cost-benefit test, it will always be optimal to accept present risks to life that will reduce comparable future risks by a small amount.[32]

If, instead, one considers the welfare of future generations, and not just the number of people alive, then one can avoid this extreme result. As Samida and Weisbach point out, treating all generations as equally worthy is not the same thing as putting aside the same amount of money in the present for all generations.[33] The present generation must only put aside enough so that compound interest will produce an amount equal to what it has kept for itself. It is one thing to value all generations equally in the social-welfare calculation and quite another to use a discount rate of zero when evaluating the value of saved lives and morbidity. The former assumes a policy goal and asks the state to achieve it by means of choices that take account of the opportunity cost of capital to investors. The latter takes the choice of a discount rate to reflect the social values of benefits and costs occurring at different points in time. If we assume a civilization of infinite (or at least several centuries) duration, with no irrevers-

---

[31] *See e.g.*, Richard L. Revesz, *Environmental Regulation, Cost-Benefit Analysis, and the Discounting of Human Lives*, 99 COLUM. L. REV. 941(1999).

[32] John Graham provides an example of the absurdities that can result. *See* Graham, *supra* note 3, at 442–47.

[33] *See* Samida & Weisbach, *supra* note 23, at 145.

ible links between catastrophe risks and today's policies, then the interests of the future are reflected in the discount rates that exist at present. However, two problems remain: converting wellbeing to a metric that can be measured and compared and dealing with the possibility of catastrophic, irreversible downside risks.

As to the former, Louis Kaplow has tried to get around this problem by assuming that utility at any point in time can be converted to dollars, discounted back to the present at the opportunity cost of capital, and then compared with a similarly monetized value for present lives.[34] That technique is consistent with the Samida and Weisbach approach, but it downplays the problem of making the required conversion. There would be no difficulty if we could assume that different generations are essentially similar on average, that we only care about the average, and that the distortions introduced to the welfare measure by using a monetary proxy are not so severe as seriously to skew the ranking of options. Furthermore, there must not be important irreversibilities that threaten overall wellbeing in a way that cannot be balanced by other compensating measures. Unfortunately, even if the other assumptions hold, the issue of climate change and other large-scale risks do not satisfy the irreversibility condition. For such issues, one should not waste time worrying about problems that arise in ordinary policy analytic exercises.

If catastrophic and irreversible harms are possible, then conventional cost-benefit analysis is not an appropriate tool. If our present actions increase the chances of a global disaster, this behavior will show up in the long-run rate of interest. The rate on long-run investments ought to rise to reflect that risk so that the certainty equivalents of different investments are kept in line. The supply of funds ought to shrink for projects that will only pay off in the distant future. Those shifts might be sufficient to persuade the government to initiate policies to limit those risks,

---

[34] *See* Kaplow, *supra* note 23, at 79.

but note that, because of the logic of discounting, very long-run harms will have little impact on current markets. The debate ought not to be framed as a debate over the discount rate.[35] Rather, it concerns the obligations of the present towards the future. Some economic analysts have dismissed this concern with the claim that future generations will be richer than we are and so we need not worry about them, beyond the incentives for saving and investment given by market interest rates and inter-familiar affection. Today, the ground has shifted as climate change and other risks appear to threaten future generations' hold on prosperity. We can still use economics to discuss the cost-effective ways to deal with climate change, but it is not going to resolve the basic issue.

CONCLUSION

The controversy over the use of cost-benefit analysis to make and assess regulatory policy has generated heated debate in the United States. Disputants accuse each of other being illogical, elitist, unethical, or lacking in compassion. The political difficulties of making policy in areas that involve morbidity and mortality are either used to justify the rejection of economic analysis or to argue for reliance on impartial expertise instead of mere political rhetoric. CBA is undermined by claims that it is biased in favor of the wealthy and of business. Alternatively, some urge that it can counter the impact of narrow interests by incorporating a comprehensive list of costs and benefits. This controversy may be repeated in France as it adopts Impact Analysis for draft

---

[35] As it is in many of the contributions to the *University of Chicago Law Review* symposium on intergenerational equity and discounting. *See, e.g.,* Sunstein & Rowell, *supra* note 23, at 171; Viscusi, *supra* note 23, at 209.

legislation and begins to systematically measure benefits and costs.

The debate often obscure the normative underpinning for cost-benefit analysis—a technique for "project" choice in the public sector that seeks to analogize those choices to the ones made by business firms picking profitable projects. The difference is that, instead of profits, the criterion of choice is overall net social benefit, but the principle is the same. One should discount all future benefits and costs for focused regulatory and spending programs that correct market failures in the near to medium term. As required by the French Organic Law, the government should be transparent about its modeling and measurement choices; it should use a sensitivity analysis to see if decisions involving these variables matter to the final outcome. Measurement issues arise in applying the net-benefit criterion, but such concerns do not challenge the basic appropriateness of CBA as a normative principle.

However, if the social choice cannot be characterized as a "project" or as a policy whose implications are small relative to the society as a whole, then CBA is not an appropriate tool. One should not force cost-benefit analysis to perform tasks for which it is, in principle, not suited. Those include policies which serve other goals, such as fairness, protection of fundamental rights, or poverty alleviation, and those that have macroeconomic consequences that are large, multigenerational, and potentially irreversible. In such cases, economic analysts can help to frame cost-effectiveness studies and to assure that policymakers include all the opportunity costs and secondary benefits. However, the ultimate policy choices must be made on other grounds. System-wide costs and benefits that accumulate over time can change the fundamental character of society; prices and other background conditions cannot be taken as given. Then policy analysis treads on the turf of economic-growth analysis and of political philosophy. It must confront the future of a society over a long time frame. The debate over climate change policy and its intersection with analyses of economic growth has highlighted the necessity of taking this perspective. Because climate change could produce catastrophic irreversibilities where the gainers from inaction in the present cannot compensate the losers in the future, ordinary attempts to incorporate the future through interest rates and discounting do not capture the essence of the problem. The logic of discounting, where a small investment today grows by compound interest to a massive sum centuries hence, is irrelevant if there might be few people in existence to enjoy the benefits. If that possibility is simply accepted as given by the present generation, the value of investing will eventually fall, and the present generation, seeing catastrophe looming for its children and grandchildren, will fail to save and invest. This may be a self-fulfilling prophecy for the kinds of society-wide risks that could appear on the horizon in the absence of action in the relatively near future.

French efforts to move the lawmaking and the regulatory process in a more functional direction, based on quantitative analysis, are positive developments. However, these steps need to be taken with an understanding of the difference between unproblematic reforms and controversial choices with normative implications. Simply outlining the benefits and costs of a new policy seems an unproblematic advance, although the requirement will, of course, highlight the lack of quantitative criteria for some polices. Most of the impacts of a new organization of the energy market or the reform of the pension system can be quantified, but those of a law restricting the wearing of the burka cannot.[36] Analysts outside the government can critique the qual-

---

[36] The French Impact Assessments are available at: http://www.legifrance. gouv.fr/html/etudes_impact/accueil.html. The IA for the pension law is "Project de loi organique relative à la limite d'âge des magistrats de l'ordre judiciare: Etude d'impact, Juillet 2010, available at: http://www.assemblee-na-tionale.fr/13/projets/pl2760-ei.asp. The IA for the burka law is "Project d'loi

ity of a quantitative IA by reanalyzing the data, as happened for energy market reorganization.[37] For an issue not suited to technocratic assessment, the political debate must occur along other dimensions. When good data are available, aggregating them to find the policy that maximizes net benefit implies a normative commitment to economic efficiency with respect to a particular policy area, such as anti-trust, pollution externalities, or natural monopoly regulation. In other policy areas such as those that deal with the redistribution of income, aid to the needy, the protection of rights, or benefits to future generation, the net benefit maximizing norm is controversial and may not even be well defined. Even in such cases IA, as required by the Organic Law can be an aid to rational policymaking, but it simply provides a framework. It is a complement, not a substitute for informed political judgment.

---

interdisant la dissimulation du visage dans l'espace public: Etude d'impact, Mai 2010, at ; http://www.legifrance.gouv.fr/html/actualite/actualite_legislative/EI_dissimulation_visage.pdf.
Its adequacy was challenged, but it was upheld by the Constitutional Council. The IA for the energy market is "Project d'loi portant nouvelle organization du marché de l'électricité (NOME): Etude d'impact," Avril 2010, at: http://www.assemblee-nationale.fr/13/projets/pl2451-ei.asp.

[37] For one critique see François Lévêque et Marcelo Saguan, "Analyse Critique de l'Etude d'Impact de la Loi NOME," Working Paper 2010-09, Cerna, Centre d'éconmie industrielle, MINES Paris Tech, June 2010: http://www.cerna.ensmp.fr/images/stories/CritiqueImpact.pdf.

CHAPTER IV

PROGRESS AND CHALLENGES IN SELECTED OECD AND EU COUNTRIES IN DEVELOPING AND USING REGULATORY IMPACT ASESSMENT (RIA)

Edward Donelan*

* M.A., Barrister at Law, Kings Inns, Dublin, Middle Temple, London, Senior Adviser, SIGMA (a joint initiative between the OECD and the European Commission), prior to his work in SIGMA he was a parliamentary counsel in Ireland for 25 years, holding a number of posts in the Office of the Attorney General, Dublin, including Director of Statute Law Revision. The views expressed are personal. This paper is a more comprehensive statement of a presentation made at Science Po, Paris at a seminar on Economic Analysis of Public Law and Policy 24/11/2010.

CONTENTS

I. Development of Policies Internationally to Improve the Quality of Government Regulation . . 127

II. Overview of the Development of the European Union Better (Now Smart) Regulation Policy . . 129

III. Use of Better Regulation Tools (Impact Assessment) 131

IV. The Essence of the RIA Framework 132

V. Advantages of the RIA Framework 134

VI. Why Impact Assessment Has Been Adopted by So Many Countries 134

VII. Does Adoption Mean Implementation? 136

VIII. Mixed Progress in Implementation 138

IX. General Conclusions 140

X. Particular Conclusions 141

THE purpose of this paper is to share some observations made over the last decade working with better regulation policies in Ireland, the new EU Member States, candidates and potential candidates to the European Union and countries to which the European Neighbourhood policy applies.

The paper provides an overview of the development of policies to improve the quality of government regulation, the development of the European Union better (now smart) regulation policy, in particular, as regards the use of better regulation tools, one of which is impact assessment. It traces the origins of impact assessment and illustrates why impact assessment has been adopted by so many countries and the processes followed in that adoption. It concludes with some key issues to be considered by developing and transition countries in the adoption and use of impact assessment as a policy tool.

I. DEVELOPMENT OF POLICIES INTERNATIONALLY TO IMPROVE THE QUALITY OF GOVERNMENT REGULATION

In March 1995, the Council of the OECD adopted a *Recommendation on Improving the Quality of Government Regulation*, which referred to the use of regulatory impact assessment (RIA). In 1997 ministers of member countries endorsed the OECD Report on Regulatory Reform, which recommended that governments "integrate regulatory impact assessment into the development, review and reform of regulations."

The origins of *RIA* can be traced to the USA. Since 1981, the Office of Information and Regulatory Affairs (OIRA) in the White House has reviewed significant proposed and final regulations for conformity with cost-benefit tests. Under a series of executive orders, OIRA has performed this role through Republican and Democratic presidencies.[1]

The adoption of RIA was in response to a perceived increase of the regulatory burden associated with a surge in regulatory activities since the mid 1960's. This perception was accompanied by concerns that the increase in regulation was adding to inflationary pressures.[2] Since 1995, the Office of Management and Budget (OMB) has been required to report on the costs and benefits of government regulations. The process has been continually improved but is still developing.[3]

---

[1] See elsewhere in this publication *Putting Cost-Benefit Analysis in Its Place: Rethinking Regulatory Review*. In her article, Professor Susan Rose- Ackermann challenges the limitations of cost benefits analysis which are a timely reminder to the assumption that impact assessment is a form of cure for all policy ills.

[2] See Anderson, J.E. (1998) 'The Struggle to Reform Regulatory Procedures, 1978 -1998', Political Studies Journal 26 (3) 482 -98. See also, for a good overview of these developments, (2007) ed., Kirkpatrick, C. and Parker, D., *Regulatory Impact Assessment: Towards Better Regulation; (2007) George*, C. and Kirkpatrick, C., *Impact Assessment and Sustainable Development*

[3] For more on this see the papers of Professor Rose-Ackermann and Professor Ogus. Also of interest is that OIRA recently added to its website a helpful checklist for use by agencies in producing regulatory impact analyses (RIAs), as required for "economically significant" regulations by Executive Order 12866 and OMB Circular A-4. The checklist does not alter, add to, or reformulate existing requirements in any way; however, it does provide a short, more easily digestible summary of those requirements. See: http://www. whitehouse.gov/sites/default/files/omb/inforeg/regpol/RIA_Checklist.pdf.

II. OVERVIEW OF THE DEVELOPMENT OF THE EUROPEAN UNION BETTER (NOW SMART[4]) REGULATION POLICY

The European Union better regulation policy has developed as a result of recognition by countries in the European Union that, to develop competitiveness, improve social welfare and protect the environment, it is necessary to have a good regulatory environment. Effective and efficient regulation is essential to correct market failures, increase competition and protect citizens, consumers, workers and the environment.

It is now well - settled that bad regulation generates unnecessary burdens on those being regulated and can create barriers to efficient markets. This, in turn, has negative impacts on competition and innovation and, in many cases, can lead to unfair income and wealth distribution. Badly designed regulation may be unenforceable, leading to non-compliance by those it is designed to regulate and a loss of credibility for public regulatory bodies.

In the last decade, EU institutions pursued three overriding objectives. The first of these was the modernisation of the European economies to boost competitiveness. This led to the Lisbon Strategy, which sought to simplify the regulatory environment and to rationalise the transposition of community legislation. The second objective was the pursuit of sustainable development. The third objective was the achievement of good governance to achieve better legitimacy, efficiency and credibility of community action. This led to a number of initiatives which included

---

[4] See Com (2010) 543 Final Communication from Commission on Smart Regulation in the EU which now focuses on: Improving the stock of EU legislation; *Simplifying EU legislation and reducing administrative burdens; Evaluating benefits and costs of existing legislation;* Ensuring that new legislation is the best possible; Improving the implementation of EU legislation; Making legislation clearer and more accessible; Improved consultation

the establishment of an expert group to develop a policy for better regulation.[5]

The Göteborg European Council (June 2001) and the Laeken European Council (December 2001) introduced two political considerations:

- To consider the effects of policy proposals in their economic, social and environmental dimensions; and
- To simplify and improve the regulatory environment in the EU.

As agreed at the Göteborg and Laeken European Councils in 2002, the Commission established a new method for impact assessment, which integrated and replaced the previously used single-sector type assessments. This method follows an integrated approach which assesses the potential impacts of new legislation or policy proposals in economic, social and environmental fields.

This new impact assessment system is an action of the Better Regulation Action Plan and of the European Strategy for Sustainable Development and, later, the Lisbon Strategy for growth and jobs (2005).[6]

It consists of a balanced appraisal of all impacts, and is underpinned by the principle of proportionate analysis, whereby the depth and scope of an impact assessment, and hence the resources allocated to it, are proportionate to the expected nature of the proposal and its likely impacts. Wide-ranging consultation with stakeholders is an integral part of the impact assessment process.

---

[5] The so called Mandelkern group named after its chairman

[6] *ec.europa.eu/governance/impact/index_en.htm*

Impact assessment in the European Commission is subject to a process of continuous improvement. The Guidelines for preparing impact assessment were revised in 2009[7] based on:
- Experience of the Commission services in preparing impact assessments
- Experience of the independent Impact Assessment Board since it was created in late 2006
- Inputs from the High Level Group of National Experts on Better Regulation
- External evaluation of the Commission's impact assessment system in 2006/2007, and
- Public consultation on the Impact Assessment Guidelines held in mid-2008.

III. USE OF BETTER REGULATION TOOLS (IMPACT ASSESSMENT)

RIA is an internationally recognised tool used in many OECD and EU countries[8] to help government officials improve policy-making by providing a framework for the assessment of policy options in terms of costs, benefits and risks. The primary motivator for the introduction of impact assessment is the need for evidence-based policy-making.

Regulatory Impact Analysis is a tool used for the structured exploration of different options to address particular policy issues. It is used where one or more of these options is a new regulation or a regulatory change and facilitates the active consideration of alternatives to regulation or lighter forms of regula-

[7] These Guidelines replace the previous Guidelines 2005 and also the 2006 update.
[8] It is also used by the Commission of the European Union

tion. It involves a detailed analysis to ascertain whether or not different options, including regulatory ones, would have the desired impact. It helps to identify any possible side effects or hidden costs associated with regulation and to quantify the likely costs of compliance on the individual citizen or business. It also helps to clarify the costs of enforcement for the State.

There is no single generic model of RIA used internationally but RIAs tend to include:
- A clear identification of objectives,
- Structured consultation with stakeholders,
- Detailed examination of impacts and consideration of the use of alternatives to regulation.

IV. THE ESSENCE OF THE RIA FRAMEWORK

The essence of the RIA framework is a series of questions, a method for calculating costs and benefits, a set of criteria for the selection of regulations or draft regulations for impact assessment and a policy on what impacts are to be assessed (economic, social, environmental and so on). Typical questions asked are:
1. Is the problem correctly defined?
2. Is government action justified?
3. Is regulation the best form of government action?
4. Is there a legal basis for regulation?
5. What is the appropriate level for government action?
6. Do the benefits justify the costs?
7. Is the distribution effect across society justified?
8. Is regulation clear, consistent, comprehensible and accessible to users?
9. Have all interested parties had the opportunity to express their views?

10. How will compliance be achieved?

The RIA process includes assessment of the costs and benefits of each of the options being considered. In addition to economic costs and benefits, it also encourages officials concerned with policy-making to examine issues such as environmental impacts and social impacts, for example improvements to health or quality of life. The effects on businesses, citizens and social groups are assessed. The aim is to provide a holistic picture of the likely effects of a proposal.

Typically, RIA goes through a number of stages. These include:

- An **initial** RIA provides a preliminary assessment that helps to expose gaps in knowledge and assists in the collection of fuller, more accurate information. Although it is largely an internal, working document, it also provides a helpful framework for discussion when taking early, informal soundings with both colleagues in other departments and external stakeholders who may be affected;
- A **partial** RIA contains more detailed policy options, with estimates of costs and benefits, as well as consideration of how each option would be implemented and enforced to ensure that a workable solution is proposed. This RIA can be used for formal public consultations with those who will be regulated and external experts;
- A **final** RIA should summarise and reflect the outcomes of consultation and make a recommendation for the course of action to be taken. It should be sent to the Cabinet and then to Parliament with legislative proposals, as it provides a useful summary of the issues and evidence to support the recommended option.

V. ADVANTAGES OF THE RIA FRAMEWORK

Using RIA properly adds a rigor to the policy-making process and can increase transparency of the decision making process through better consultation. In this latter regard, RIA is also a valuable communication tool. It can be used to:
- Describe and explain the rationale for government intervention,
- Collect and articulate the evidence for proposals, and
- Facilitate consultation in policy-making.

RIA can also be used to summarise and consultations that have taken place in the policy cycle and set out how this has influenced the final policy choice. [9]

VI. WHY IMPACT ASSESSMENT HAS BEEN ADOPTED BY SO MANY COUNTRIES

It could be argued that RIA has been introduced as a result of successive OECD reports into regulatory reforms. [10] These reports have promoted the idea of regulatory impact assessment

---

[9] See sigmaweb.org and various presentations (Croatia, Egypt, Georgia, Jordan, and Turkey) by Karen Hill, UK, regulatory reform expert. Ms Hill played a leading role in the development of better regulation policies in the UK and in recent years has enjoyed a successful career as an independent consultant working in a range of countries to develop impact assessment and improve regulation. See also *www.mof.gov.eg/.../English/ERRADA%20Newsletter%20Jul%2010.pdf*

[10] *OECD Principles for Regulatory Quality and Performance* (OECD, 2005) call on countries to "integrate RIA in the development, review and revision of significant regulations", as well as to "ensure that RIA plays a key role in improving the quality of regulation, and is conducted in a timely, clear and transparent manner."

and have argued persuasively that the introduction of RIA brings about many benefits[11]. Essentially, these benefits are:

- *RIA requires decisions to be taken with much stronger rigour and through a more accountable and transparent process.* The systematic process of questioning at the beginning of the policy cycle facilitates reflection on how to structure the policy-making process, identify cause-effect links and likely impacts, select and compare policy options, and consider unintended consequences. This helps reduce the risk of regulatory failures.

- *RIA allows for an outward-looking, decision-making process.* If properly integrated with public consultation and if published in a timely and systematic way, RIAs empower economic operators and citizens and respond to their right to know the reasons for policy and regulatory choices. This contributes to minimising regulatory capture. Three immediate consequences flow from this: a more stable recognition and generalised acceptance of the performance of policy-makers; greater trust in public authorities; and higher compliance rates with regulation.

- *RIA helps shift from a legalistic to a more evidence-based approach to decision-making.* RIA facilitates co-ordination between different public policies, with an aim of highlighting trade-offs and identifying synergies. This helps achieve greater policy coherence; break down sectoral approaches and promote 'horizontal' thinking – contributing thereby to limiting regulatory inflation.[12]

---

[11] Interestingly, this theme is picked up elsewhere in this publication and Martina Conticelli
Assistant Professor in Public Law, University of Rome Tor Vergata explores the influence of international organisations in her paper: *Assessing National Reforms through Global Indicators*

[12] Overview of European Practices for Assessing Impacts of proposed Policies, presentation at a Workshop: Introduction to Regulatory Impact Assessment, Tbilisi, 20th July 2010, Lorenzo Allio (see www.sigmaweb.org). Fol-

VII. DOES ADOPTION MEAN IMPLEMENTATION?

The widespread adoption of RIA is beyond doubt.[13] However, adoption does not mean implementation. Experience suggests that RIA must undergo much iteration before it is embedded fully in the policy-making process of a country.[14]

The success or failure of RIA in any given country depends on the institutional arrangements, the amount of political support and the manner in which impact assessment was adopted. In the SIGMA study of the regulatory management capacities of the new member states[15] what was observed was that many countries had adopted laws which mandated RIA but few had put the necessary structures or personnel in place to do them properly.

Similar findings have been made by OECD and other studies. Radaelli (2005) for instance speaks of "diffusion without convergence"[16]. Another study suggests that the motivation to

---

lowing a period working with the OECD Dr. Allio is now and independent policy analyst and consultant who has advised a wide range of governments.

[13] OECD (2009), *Indicators of Regulatory Management Systems*, Paris

[14] See, for example, In July 2008, the Department of the Taoiseach (Prime Minister in Ireland) published a review it had commissioned on the implementation of RIA in Ireland (Goggin and Lauder, 2008). The Review examined the extent to which Departments and Offices were meeting the requirement to produce RIAs and assessed the effectiveness of the supports available to officials conducting RIAs. In overall terms it concluded that, while good progress has been made, further work was needed to ensure that, when RIAs are carried-out, they contain sufficiently detailed analysis, that there is sufficient consultation and that they are published. See presentations by Mr. T. Ferris at various SIGMA workshops in Cairo, Tbilisi, Zagreb etc www.sigmaweb.org Mr. Ferris, a former Chief Economist at the Ministry of Transport in Ireland is now an independent consultant and has worked in a variety of countries for the OECD and the World Bank.

[15] New member states are those that joined on and after the 1st May 2004. See SIGMA paper No 42 www.sigmaweb.org

[16] Radaelli, C.M. (2005), "Diffusion without convergence: how political context shapes the adoption of regulatory impact assessment", in *Journal of European Public Policy*, Vol.12/5, p.924-943.

enhance market regulation efficiency is not always the main rationale for adopting RIA. Governments adopt RIA (or forms of it) under the pressure of various drivers, including political control and social legitimacy rather than efficiency.[17] To this one could add my own observations about the adoption of RIA in Ireland followed the OECD review of regulatory reform in Ireland, there was no domestic demand for such a policy tool. The main driver for the reform was the OECD report and the view of some senior officials that the introduction of RIA would be beneficial.

There is a further argument put forward by a well- known expert in the field [18]that there are many difficulties in implementing RIA. The adoption of RIA "is not a linear upward trend, but actually follows a U-shaped curve. In the early years, relatively few RIAs are conducted, but are conducted under the scrutiny of a small cadre of RIA experts. As RIA becomes integrated into general policy processes, it is carried out by a larger and larger group of people with fewer skills. In this period of expansion, the quality of RIA seems to be declining. At some stage, the consolidation stage, the training and other quality control mechanisms catch up with the expansion, and the quality of RIA begins to rise again."

[17] EVIA (2008), *Improving the Practice of Impact Assessment*, Policy Paper, February.

[18] Scott Jacobs now with Jacobs and Associates; regulatory Reform was the driver behind the OECD reports on regulatory reform in many countries. These reports influenced the development of RIA. See: Jacobs, S. (2006), *Current Trends in Regulatory Impact Analysis: The Challenges of Mainstreaming RIA into Policy-making*, Jacobs and Associates, Washington.

VIII. MIXED PROGRESS IN IMPLEMENTATION

This pattern of adoption but not implementation was observed by SIGMA in its review of the new member states.[19] Since that review further work is being done by those countries to embed RIA more effectively. Progress is mixed and will need to be reviewed again. Matrix Insight, a London-based public policy consultancy have recently been commissioned by the European Parliament's Directorate General for Internal Policies to conduct a study looking at the purpose, scope and procedures of Regulatory Impact Assessments (RIA) carried out in the Member States of the EU. The study will rely primarily on the synthesis and analysis of existing documentation supplemented by a set of interviews with key stakeholders in selected EU Member States. The challenge for the development of RIA in developing and transition countries is, of course, resources both human and capital.

A recent study by the OECD[20] showed how in Poland, for example, the unit in the Chancellery of the Prime Minister, which is responsible for the control of quality of impact assessments, is seriously understaffed. With only few employees, it may focus only on assessing formal aspects of impact assessments

In Poland, implementation of the Regulatory Impact Assessment (RIA) was initiated at the end of 2001. Since that time, it has been mandatory to carry out impact assessment studies for all governmental legal acts. The system of regulatory impact assessment covers both bills and regulations.

---

[19] SIGMA Paper No 42 Regulatory Management in New EU Member States, (Donelan, E) www.sigmaorg.com

[20] Not yet published and subject to further review (November 2010)

RIA is mandated by a law[21] which requires a summary of RIA results to be attached explanatory notes published with legislation. The RIA statement should identify parties affected by the regulation, present the results of public consultations, identify impacts that the regulation will have on public finances including central and local budgets, labour market, internal and external competitiveness, regions and regional development and indicate sources of funding. The structure of the RIA final report, according to the Guidelines prepared by Ministry of Economy, should comprise the following items:

- Problem analysis with brief description of the issue;
- Aim, effects, and circumstance containing the purpose of the proposed regulation and background information on existing legal framework and justification of the change along with risk assessment;
- Options with brief description of how the available intervention options including a resignation from public intervention and intervention other than legislative.
- Consultation with brief description how consultation was planned and carried out and the way in which consultation results were used in the assessment of regulation impact;
- Costs and benefits;
- Subjects to be affected by the regulation;
- Detailed analysis of the costs and benefits resulting from the options and presented in a table of costs and benefits for the subjects and areas of public finance, labour market, competitiveness and entrepreneurship, impact on regional development and environmental impact;
- Implementation, enforcement, monitoring;
- Recommended option;
- Implementation plan.

---

[21] Ordinance No. 49 of the Council of Ministers from March 19, 2002 – Rules of Procedures of Council of Ministers

Impact assessment is performed for all draft regulations in Poland, whatever their nature and impact as long as they are subject to obligatory promulgation in Polish official journals. However, the RIA system is not applied to EU Regulations (other than EU Directives to be transposed, RIA is not carried out when the EU proposal for a Regulation is under discussion by the EU institutions).

Following the SIGMA report on the Regulatory Management Capacities of the New Member States, fresh Guidelines on Regulatory Impact Assessment were approved by the Council of Ministers in 2006. Institutional arrangements for RIA have been implemented in 2006 in order to strengthen the RIA system, including placing responsibility for the review of RIA in the Chancellery of the Prime Minister instead of the Government Legislation Centre where it was until July 2006. At present, the Chancellery of the Prime Minister indicates whether the scope of the assessment is adequate and identifies the elements which the ministry should apply to expand the impact assessment and make it as complete as possible. The Chancellery does not have a right to veto proposals that do not contain sufficient assessment of regulatory impacts.

IX. GENERAL CONCLUSIONS

RIA is a structured process for considering the implications, for people and their environment, of proposed actions while there is still an opportunity to modify (or even, if appropriate, abandon) the proposals. It is applied at all levels of decision-making, from policies to specific projects. The process involves the identification and characterisation of the most likely impacts of proposed actions (impact prediction/forecasting) and an assessment of the social significance of these impacts (impact evaluation).

The use of impact assessment is a consequence of governments in OECD and EU countries and the institutions of the European Union becoming more conscious of the need to improve governance and the quality of policy-making and law drafting. Progress towards its adoption and implementation has been slow and there is no one model that works so well that it can be followed by transitional or developing countries. Each country has to review what has been done in other countries and develop a process and institutional arrangements that best suit its own structure and conditions.

X. PARTICULAR CONCLUSIONS

SIGMA has just finished a project in Croatia to initiate the development of RIA in that country. The process included a series of awareness- building workshops, the appointment of a group of people in that country to develop a model and a final conference to launch the process, which was attended by the Deputy Prime Minister and almost all the heads of Ministries. The next step for Croatia will be an EU Twinning Project[22] which will help broaden and deepen the reform. Similar work will be undertaken by SIGMA in Egypt, Georgia and Jordan.

---

[22] Twinning is a European Commission initiative that was originally designed to help candidate countries acquire the necessary skills and experience to adopt, implement and enforce EU legislation. Since 2003, twinning has been available to some of the Newly Independent States of Eastern Europe and to countries of the Mediterranean region. It involves a senior official from a member state of the EU spending a period of time working in a country and helping build capacity in a particular area.

From these projects, my conclusions about the key issues to be considered by developing and transition countries in the adoption and use of impact assessment as a policy tool are that:

1. Political support is essential not just for the establishment of the policy but for its development and continual improvement.
2. The selection of a good team to initiate the process is crucial. The team should be multidisciplinary (administrators, policy-makers, lawyers and an economist) at the centre to provide Ministries with support and to review the quality of impact assessments when made.
3. Resources must be made available.
4. Links must be built with a University and a good firm of economists to provide training and support.
5. All concerned must be prepared for a process of improvement and time must be allowed for training and communicating the message that RIA makes for better policies.

CHAPTER V

ASSESSING NATIONAL REFORMS THROUGH GLOBAL INDICATORS. CASE STUDY

MARTINA CONTICELLI*

* Assistant Professor in Public Law, University of Rome Tor Vergata.

CONTENTS

I. The Object and the Purpose of this Study 145

II. Global Institutions Concerning National Administrative Reform Policies 148

III. The Reasons for a Global Concern Over a National Phenomenon 150

IV. The Dimension of the Concern Under an Organizational Perspective 155

V. The Method, the Object and the Priorities in Global Assessment Over National Administrative Reform Policies 158

VI. Final Considerations 160

I. THE OBJECT AND THE PURPOSE OF THIS STUDY

THIS paper investigates the extra-national dimension of policy assessment, focusing on the evaluation of national administrative reform policies at the global level.[1] As many other public functions, policy assessment, as well, no longer has a purely national character: differently from other fields of intervention, however, in this case the implications of globalization on this function are not clearly evident. On the one hand, this is due to the bias according to which globalization should not affect administrative systems, nor should global institutions' decisions be able to produce direct effects on national administrations. On the other hand, this is a natural consequence of the circumstance that global policy assessment implies considering administrative systems as economic goods or commodities.

We argue that the object of this study is a privileged field of investigation to question both these views: dealing with it not only allows us to experiment with the global dimension of public administration and activity, but it also provides us with the basis for combining the economic perspective of globalization together with the legal one.

---

[1] For an overview on the use of indicators in the global legal system, see the papers discussed at the Institute for international law and justice conference on *Indicators as a Technology of Global Governance*, September 13-14, 2010. For an italian perspective of the impact of global regulation on administrative reforms, see M. D'Alberti, *Riforme amministrative e sistema economico*, Relazione presentata al Convegno su *Il sistema amministrativo a dieci anni dalla riforma Bassanini*, Roma 30 gennaio 2008, dattiloscritto.

We start with the premise that the relationship between what we could merely refer to as globalization and administrative reform policy is a complex one. The two contemporary phenomena have much in common: to begin with, they both came about during the 20th century. Globalization arises immediately after World War II, it develops before the end of the century, finally becoming, at the beginning of the 21st century, one of the main features of the contemporary world. A similar evolution can be followed in reference to administrative reforms, which, as noted by the legal doctrine,[2] developed in the course of the 20th century, and yet by the end of it, ceased to be isolated events, markedly defining their independence from other public policies.

It is common knowledge that, thanks to globalization, national administrations come in contact with other global actors, both public and private ones. There can also be no doubt of the fact that, by stimulating the intervention of national governments, globalization has a proactive effect on reforms operating in many fields in administrative law.[3] What is less clear, and to what more attention will be given here, is the interest of global powers on the real impact of such a process. This can be discussed through the examination of the follow-up phase of the whole assessment process, which might be considered here not only under a procedural perspective (as the monitoring process and the subsequent assessment of national administrative reforms by the global

[2] In the words used with reference to administrative reforms by S. Cassese, *L'età delle riforme amministrative*, Riv. trim. dir. pubbl., 2001, p. 80.

[3] See S. Cassese e M. Savino, *The Global Economy, Accountable Governance, and Administrative Reform*, discussion paper for the *6th Global Forum on Reinventing Government Towards Participatory and Transparent Governance*, Seoul, 2004, p. 3.

actors),[4] but which will be discussed in terms of its relevance both within national legal orders and in the global one.[5]

Continuing from this premise, an estimation of the real impact of the global assessment on national administrative reform policy is required, which gives rise to a series of preliminary questions.

The first issue to the supra-national organisations, that is to say, the global bodies and their areas of their concern. Who, in the global legal arena, should be concerned with national administrative reforms, and to what extent should be global institutions be interested in domestic administrative performance?

The second set of inquiries involves mainly functional aspects. Why should ultra- national bodies concentrate on national administrative reforms?

The third issue under discussion concerns precisely the sense and menaing of the global assessment process in the global arena. How relevant is this function, and how are collecting data, monitoring procedures and assessment decision carried forward? To whom are they addressed?

The last one entails the discussion of methodological choices. What kind of assessments do global institutions carry out? On which indicators and according to which method of calculation do they fbase their evaluations? In what type of changes in ad-

---

[4] To this end, we take into account as object of this study general national administrative reform policies:we do not make reference only to the italian ones but national reforms under a more comprehensive perspective. We do not investigate reform policies which attain the organizational structure and work by International organizations.

[5] For a deeper examination and for the whole discusssion on the issue, see *Note e commenti sul sistema amministrativo italiano in contesto internazionale*, edited G. Pennella, Formez; M. Ascione e V. Russo, *Misura della performance amministrativa in un contesto internazionale di cooperazione e competizione*, Relazione al seminario di studio su *Innovazione amministrativa, contesto internazionale e crescita*, Bologna, 15 gennaio 2008; S. Salvi, M. Salvatore e A. Zuliani, *L'amministrazione pubblica italiana nel contesto competitivo europeo*, Mipa.

ministrative performance and in which areas of administrative legal systems are they most interested?

As a first impression, the relationship between globalization and administrative reform policy appears unidirectional, since it looks like it is only the former that influences the latter. Through the examination of the global assessment mechanisms we aim to give an alternative perspective, and reach a partially different conclusion, demonstrating how globalization and administrative reform policies influence each other in a mutual way.

II. GLOBAL INSTITUTIONS CONCERNING NATIONAL ADMINISTRATIVE REFORM POLICIES

Many international organizations pay attention to national administrative reform policies: the majority of them currently monitor development and carry out assessment reports. We will therefore take into consideration only a few of them, by way of example:

  a) the Organisation for Economic Co-operation and Development (hereafter OECD) releases several reports on the state of administrative reforms in Member States, some of which come out yearly;[6]

  b) the International Monetary Fund (hereafter IMF) carries out yearly meetings –not only in order to discuss about the state of national economies, but also to evaluate the development in the field of administrative reform policy,[7]

---

[6] For instance, since 2005 the release *Economic Policy Reforms: Going for Growth*, and in 2009 *Goverments at a Glance*.

[7] See, along this line, Imf, San Marino – Consultazioni ai sensi dell'articolo IV, at www.finanze.sm/, or for Switzerland, the Releases o consultations on public economy betweeen the Imf and Switzerland, on which, see: http://www.efv.admin.ch/i/themen/iwf/iwf_politik.php. As far as Italy is con-

while the World Bank (hereafter WB) occasionally sends to the Russian Federation its reports on the administrative reform techniques experimented by other countries;[8]

c) the World Trade Organization (hereinafter WTO) currently monitors, for example, the process of administrative reforms in the Republic of China (and also in other countries);

d) through their social and economic affairs Department, the United Nations (hereafter UN) collect information on administrative reforms worldwide and keep statistical data updated;

e) the World Economic Forum (hereafter WEF) and the Economist Intelligence Unit (hereafter EIU) assess the competitiveness of countries on a regular basis, founding their judgements on indicators referred to the legal environment and to the institutional context: the *Global Competitiveness Report* 2010/2011 issued by the former, for instance, places Italy as 48th in competitiveness with reference to the administrative system, called the *Public Institutions Index*; the same country is ranked in a slightly better position in the *Business Environment Ranking*, released by the latter.

The concern about the impact of national administrative reform policies is now widespread among global actors, as is proved by the fact that the outcome is of common interest to many institutions -such as those enlisted above- which differ notably among themselves in terms of their structure and membership, their mission, their tasks and their areas of work. And the complete list of actors involved would be even much longer.

---

cerned, see Italy – 2006, Imf Article IV Consultation Preliminary Conclusions of the Mission November 13, 2006.

[8] See N. Manning and N. Parison, *International Public Administration Reform. Implications for the Russian Federation*, Washington, 2003.

Nevertheless, the cases selected in this paper will explain most of the existing variations, insofar as, to begin with, they include different kind of actors: four of them are public international organizations, some are private organizations, such as WEF and EIU; some are "weak" organizations, as for instance the OECD, while others, such as the IMF and the WTO, have a strong role to play in international affairs; some of them are called to fulfil a broad mission, such as the UN and the OECD, while others work is to cover more limited areas of intervention, as for instance the WB; some, among them, are intergovernmental organization who are required to manage multiple tasks, from development, to peacekeeping and trade, while some others are non-governmental actors whose mandate is clearly defined and limited to carrying out rating reports (maybe in consultative status with the Economic and Social Council Ecosoc, of the UN).

III. THE REASONS FOR A GLOBAL CONCERN OVER A NATIONAL PHENOMENON

After accepting how widespread the attention about national administrative reform policies is, the following aspect which we need to assess is the analysis of the goals of such a process at the global level. Accordingly, at least two questions merit examination and to answer them, we need to focus again on the aforementioned examples. Why should we concern ourselves with national reforms? And –more importntly- why precisely the administrative ones?

    a) Instead of considering single countries, the OECD reports cover any Member State's legal system: yet, the analysis is restricted to those administrative reforms which have a direct impact on economic development. Despite this sector-specific approach, nevertheless, these reports give a relatively comprehensive overview of the administrative systems examined, addressing topics such as the persistence of regulatory barriers and constraints to competition; the organisation, the management and the delivery of tertiary education; or the developments in *revenue system pressures on labour income*. This is because the reform of the national regulatory framework in this case directly affects the areas covered by the OECD's mission, whose concern is justified by –but also limited to- the implementation of the task assigned: which is why the monitoring procedure, in this case, is followed by an assessment procedure.

b) More complex is the assessment process within the IMF and the WB. To begin with, differently from the OECD's case, here, data are collected and analysed separately by country. Furthermore, as far as the object of the evaluation is concerned, the IMF's assessment process reviews only those administrative reforms which have an impact on economic stability and growth, with a focus on fiscal policies and structural reforms, but also on liberalization and de-regulation,[9] while the WB takes into account only those which may affect the efficiency of administrative activity, with a focus on public expenditure arrangements, personnel management and civil service, organizational structure of the executive, role of and policy load carried by government.[10]

---

[9] See, for instance, with reference to the Italian context, Italy - 2006 IMF Article IV Consultation, Preliminary Conclusions of the Mission, November 13, 2006, where: '[g]rowth is picking up, some progress has already been achieved on the structural reform agenda, and buoyant revenues are helping the fiscal out turn. This is the most propitious economic environment in years to unshackle Italy's growth potential by putting the fiscal accounts in order, enhancing domestic competition, and improving the business environment. If not now, when?'.

[10] Within the report released for the Russia Federation, as a way of example, the World Bank took into account 14 countries, whose reforms related to

We consider that the different purposes of the two main global financial institutions influence not only the acquisition of data, but also the outcome of the assessment process, as well as the final feedback. Because of this, we need to spend a few words on this.

In the first case, a matter of membership in the organisation is under question: therefore the assessment process is aimed at checking that the high requirements imposed to partners are respected, each of which must prove the adoption of all the necessary measures to keep the competitiveness of their administrative system under control (this is particularly evident with reference to the annual consultations of the IMF with Member States).[11] The WB assessment process aims here at a completely different goal: its evaluation of a country's administrative system reveals the concern of the creditor toward the sustainability of the commitment of the debtor. Beside the mere informative aim and the demand of accomplishment of membership's institutional tasks, therefore, another purpose is revealed. We refer to the loans provided by the WB to developing countries, and to the conditional mechanism, according to which positive or negative assessment about national administrative reform policy has practical consequences.

---

the following issue has been given evidence: *Public expenditure; arrangements, personnel management and civil service, organizational structure of the executive, role of and policy load carried by government: see International Public Administration Reform. Implications for the Russian Federation*, edited by N. Manning e N. Parison, World Bank, Washington, 2003.

[11] Such consultations are mandated in Article IV of IMF Articles of Agreement. They form part of a general surveillance task aimed at keeping political, economic and financial stability in Member States under control: these are all considered as essential conditions for membership. Should a State be given a negative assessment a plan of reforms is prepared and checked during the subsequent consultations.

c) The WTO's concern about administrative change crucially depends on whether the reform under examination is that of an existing Member State or of a State desiring to become a member. In the former case, administrative reform policy becomes relevant only if it is preliminary to trade liberalization itself and only as far as it plays an influence on trade barriers reductions,[12] while, in the latter, the same policy is taken under consideration merely to evaluate the new partner's admissibility conditions.[13]

d) A completely different perspective must be adopted to explain the case of the UN, where the monitoring activity appears initially addressed to merely provide information. At a first sight, in fact, the concern over collecting data does not seem affected by other goals, as happens with the statistical systems operating at a domestic level: nevertheless, information is then useful to highlight the *best practices* in administrative systems worldwide. In other words, here we emphasise the establishment of a comparative goal, which brings new elements for evaluation into the arena. Notwithstanding this, the UN concern is not

---

[12] See, along this line, WTO News: 2004 Press Releases, Press/385, 16 September 2004, World Trade Report, where, with specific reference to the so called «Impact of Domestic Policies on Trade the Focus of 2004» we read that «[b]enefits from good trade policy may be attenuated or even undermined if governments pursue deficient policies in other areas of economic activity, according to the 2004 World Trade Report published by the WTO Secretariat», disponibile alla pagina web: http://www.wto.org/english/news_e/pres04_e/pr385_e.htm.

[13] See, Wto, General Council Meeting: 7 November 2006, Accession of Viet Nam – Report of the Working Party (WT/ACC/VNM/48 and Add. 1 and 2), where: «[t]o achieve this target, Viet Nam would speed up its economic reforms, complete a full market mechanism, improve administrative management capacity, and accelerate administrative reform and corruption eradication. Viet Nam aimed to strictly implement its WTO commitments and actively contribute to the common tasks of the WTO; it was also resolved to be a responsible and reliable Member and to contribute to a mutually beneficial, fair and balanced multilateral trading system».

embedded with any normative purpose: on the contrary, in this case, this international organisation provides Member States with a forum of debate. As a matter of fact, there is incentive for the pontaneous circulation of administrative reforms models, which acts as a *stimulus* for further reforms, without requiring or imposing any specific change or additional reform in Member States' legal orders.

e) The concern for administrative reform policies by credit rating agencies does not answer to any of the purposes pointed out so far. In their evaluation of national economies, credit rating agencies address other actors' investment choices, being they private parties or public investors. Therefore, they take into consideration only specific indicators such as –to quote only those referred to the socio-political and institutional context- the legal environment, the availability of human capital, the degree of inrastructure development and the efficiency of the administrative system.[14]

Some first conclusions might be drawn from the case study's analysis developed so far. Firstly, the examination of each institution's concern over national administrative reform policies and the investigation on the connection with their mission prove that global actors' monitoring process is multipurpose. Secondly, we argue that this has relevant implications on the procedure adopted for the assessment process: depending on the case, an audit phase may come after the monitoring one. A third observation is the following: the consequences of the whole assessment process usually affects only the relationship between the specific organization and each State, apart from the last case, where the

---

[14] Ne riferiscono A. Zuliani e S. Salvi, in *Note e commenti sul sistema amministrativo italiano in contesto internazionale*, Formez, p. 24-25.

results of the evaluation by credit rating agencies have a weight on strategic choices of third parties as investors.

IV. THE DIMENSION OF THE CONCERN UNDER AN ORGANIZATIONAL PERSPECTIVE

On first impression, international bureaucracies should mostly be employed in collecting data and information: this is certainly true if we refer to information in general. A part of this activity is focused on national administrative reform policies. However, only in a few cases this task is clearly defined and put under the responsibility of a specific single unit.

As a way of example, the institutions which we have been dealing with adopt various organizational arrangements for the delivering of the final assessment. We argue that the more is the institution concerned in the implementation of this task, the more is the connected structural asset developed.

a) Among those discussed here, the OECD is concerned with administrative reform policies, perhaps more than other organizations, due to its close connection with innovation, growth and development: the main tasks related to this activity are concentrated in a specific single unit, such as the *Public Governance and Territorial Development Directorate.*

b) The same area of tasks is spread across three units within the IMF. The *Policy Development and Review Department*, the *Research Department* and the *Statistics Department* collect and analyse data. Also, they share this responsibility with other units. As far as the WB is concerned, apart from the *Information Officer*, monitoring tasks are carried out by any of its units according to each area of competences which they are instrumental to.

c) Within the organizational structure of the WTO, most of the monitoring and reporting on statistical data over national administrations are provided by the *Economic Research and Statistic Division*, which is part of the secretariat and comes under a deputy director general.[15] Along with this division, other units collect information and deliver reports as a way to implement technical assistance: here the information activity is clearly instrumental to comply with the tasks assigned. This is the case, for instance, of the *Institute for Training and Technical Cooperation*, whose mandate is focused on helping developing countries, lesser-developed ones and other low-income transition economies to mainstream trade into their national economic development plans and strategies, through the release of periodical surveys.

d) Considerable attention is paid to monitoring national administrative reform policies within the organizational structure of the UN: here the tasks related fall under the responsibility of a special unit, which comes under the *Division for Public Administration and Development Management* of the *Department of Economic and Social Affairs*, the so-called *United Nations Online Network in Public Administration and Finance* (UNPAN).

e) The delivery of assessment through the *Global Competitiveness Report* released by the WEF, on the contrary, as the collection of data on national administrations is carried out by the *Centre for Global Competitiveness and Performance*. This unit works together with experts, leading economists and academics worldwide, who are occasionally called to cooperate under the direction of the heads

---

[15] This Unit comes as third for dimension, sources and employees, preceded only by the Languages Documentation and Information Management Division and by the Administration and General Services Division.

of the non-governmental organization. Besides professionals, also national governments, public administrations, and private undertakings are involved in the assessment process, being requested to give information.

The various allocations chosen for the assessment process within the organizational structure of the global institutions examined suggest how different is the weight assigned to evaluating national administrative reform policy. Any time informative purposes prevail against other goals of public interest the monitoring and reporting tasks are clearly identified and usually fall under the area of responsibility of special units, on a functional basis. On the contrary, when the release of surveys and in general the assessment process have other implications (such as for conditional mechanisms) or when information is preliminary to the accomplishment of other goals within the mandate of the institution itself, the related task are assigned to those units responsible to perform with the main function to which information is related, on an instrumental basis.

One last remark we might add as far as the latest case is concerned, in order to explain the involvement of external experts. The need for external expertise here depends on the fact that the outcome is addressed to third parties and influences their view, instead of being limited to the institution itself. Accordingly, participation finds a justification in a claim for legitimacy, since the main consequences of the assessment process here affect the general opinion on a specific country, operating out of any specific relationship between this latter and the agency

V. THE METHOD, THE OBJECT AND THE PRIORI-TIES IN GLOBAL ASSESSMENT OVER NATIONAL ADMINISTRATIVE REFORM POLICIES

Consistent with the main conclusions reached so far, the selection of what is considered relevant for the surveys and the choice on which method of data analysis is more appropriate are also instrumentally related to the nature of the concern and to the priorities assigned to each institution. Some evidence has been already pointed out above about the reasons for such concerns of global actors about administrative reform policies. Some other general remarks might be added now.

As far as the selection of relevant information for evaluation is concerned, apart from the case of the UN and, in a few cases, of the WB, a sector-oriented approach of analysis prevails at a global level: the policy area under assessment is strictly connected with development in the OECD case, with lowering trade barriers as a stimulus for economic growth in the case of the WTO, and with national economic stability as for the IMF and the WEF. Even if justified by the mission assigned, such an approach nevertheless provides the global institution with a partial view on administrative legal systems; the limits of such an object of assessment are self-evident, since the area under evaluation does not allow to consider properly the multiple linkages between different sectors of administrative systems,[16] and prevents the institution from

---

[16] We experiment an over-evaluation of some aspects with respect to oth-ers, similarly to what happens at the national level, but with more problematic implications, due to the sector-oriented approach of the global arena. For a discussion on this mechanism, with peculiar emphasis on the labour issue in respect of other involved functional issues even if with specific reference to the domestic legal context, see C. Franchini, *La riforma amministrativa in Ita-lia*, in S. Cassese e C. Franchini, *Tendenze recenti della riforma amministrativa in Europa*, Bologna, Il Mulino, 1989, p. 172.

taking into due consideration administrative changes as part of a whole and more complex project of reform.[17]

In a similar way, criticisms may be raised about the methods adopted for surveying, analysing and processing data: not only each institution makes its own selection on information and on areas of investigation but also, even when approaching the same issue, each of them place great emphasis on their own criteria of evaluation and their adopt their own methodology of survey. As a matter of fact, meaningful divergences arise, which affect the final outcome, and which are often non-secondary in terms of relevance.[18]As a way to partially face criticisms in advance, in some cases, institutions were accustomed to discuss at length their methodological choices with representatives from national governments and experts, as shown by the survey released by the OECD about *Towards Better Measurement of Governments* e *Towards Governments at a Glance*.

Beside the critical remarks on methodology, also a question of data sources must be raised and taken into deep account. Since they cannot count on direct information sources, global institutions choose their own ad hoc interlocutor among expert coming from the business environment, private parties, civil servants or representatives from national governments. It is needless to mention the implications this choice may have on the final outcome of their surveys.

---

[17] About the merits of a global overview on any reform project, even if with specific reference to the so called Rapporto Giannini in the Italian case, see C. Franchini, *La riforma amministrativa in Italia*, in S. Cassese and C. Franchini, *Tendenze recenti della riforma amministrativa in Europa*, Bologna, Il Mulino, 1989, p. 167 ss.

[18] For a critical opinion along such lines, see A. Zuliani, *Competizione internazionale e pubbliche amministrazioni italiane*, in *Note e commenti sul sistema amministrativo italiano in contesto internazionale*, edited by G. Pennella, Formez, 2006, p. 77 ss.

VI. FINAL CONSIDERATIONS

What conclusions may be drawn from this analysis? First of all, relevant pressures on administrative reform policy –as well as on the assessment process– also come from global institutions. As they are inspired by ideological, political or even economic concerns,[19] in any case, the need for change in administrative systems as well as the concern over policy assessment do not come anymore from central government, local government or from the same administrations involved, not only from the public sector. On the contrary, they are more and more driven by global actors, not only public organizations, but also private powers. Assessment is particularly involved, since administrative reform policies have real implications not only for national constituencies, but also for other actors operating outside the national boundaries.

Secondly, the reasons that motivate administrative change must be stressed. their recognition is relevant, since it is only on their basis that we might truly evaluate each reform policies' internal coherence. Not surprisingly, the key reasons for change usually enlisted by scholars and experts come out strengthened from the analysis of what occurs within the global arena as they are confirmed by each of the case studies discussed (even if they are taken into consideration under a sector-oriented perspective, as we have noticed).

Such a consideration is important not only in reference to internal constraints, such as the demand of rationalization of the administrative apparatus, or the need to restrain public expense, or the claim for more efficiency in administrative action, but also, and maybe more so, in reference to external pressures

---

[19] See, Y. Meny e V. Wright, *Introduzione. Le burocrazie e la sfida del cambiamento*, in *La riforma amministrativa in Europa*, edited by Y. Meny and V. Wright, il Mulino, Bologna, p. 1994.

or incentives, such as the wish to improve day-to-day relation-ships with citizens, to promote greater transparency and to cir-culate information about administrative decisions. In addition to those enlisted, peculiar calls arise at the global level, such as the need to meet the global financial institutions' requirements in order to obtain a loan, or to achieve a good evaluation by credit rating agencies' surveys, to comply with the international com-mitments, to start dealings for becoming a member of a global institution.

Thirdly, what is most interesting about the phenomenon dis-cussed here relies not as much on the fact that the during the last two decades global institutions have been showing grow-ing concern over national administrative policy reforms,[20] as in the circumstance that their interest forms part of a conditional mechanism which have concrete implications on the relation-ships between global and national legal orders.

On one side, a deep concern over the testing of administra-tive systems arises,[21] nevertheless, public administration statis-tics apparently do not receive official acknowledgement within the global legal order. Long considered as one of the main func-tions within domestic legal orders, which allocated the tasks con-nected to *ad hoc* units, a similar treatment is still not given within the global arena, where, on the contrary, public administration statistics would even be of greater importance, since the global legal order cannot count on a common heritage of information.

No institution is officially charged with the task of gathering information and reviewing data. On one side, we could argue that there has been to narrow a reading of the real dimensions of this phenomenon as well as of the need for information. On the

[20] F. Bassanini, *The dynamics of public sector reform*, Second quality Confer-ence for public administration, Copenhaghen, 2-4 ottobre 2002, disponibile all'indirizzo http://www.giustizia- amministrativa.it/ .

[21] See S. Cassese, *Che cosa vuol dire «amministrazione di risultati»?*, *Giorn. Dir. Amm.*, 2004, p. 941.

other, of course, this would require a high degree of development in the division of tasks, which is rare outside national boundaries, especially if we consider the still primitive character of the global legal arena.

At the same time, we have seen that many global institutions perform with this task without having received any specific mandate and often even in an informal way. Most of them take into consideration the same selection of data, but read from very different perspectives.

A broad range of outcomes arise, if we consider that only in the area of competitiveness assessment four reports are released: the *Global Competitiveness Report* by the WEF, the *World Competitiveness Yearbook* by the IMD Business School, the *Index of Economic Freedom* by the Heritage foundation and the *Doing Business Project* by the WB. Moreover, in most cases a partial view of each administrative system is offered; in many others, an assessment according to each institution's mission is given. As a consequence, the same administrative legal system can be ranked differently; this could probably be even acceptable, if we would not take into consideration the various practical implications these assessment may have.

On the other side, the object of the analysis is even made more problematic under the circumstance that in the global arena not only private parties are put into competition the one with the others, but also administrative legal systems are under scrutiny. Because of this, administrative reform policies have become one of the main parameters used to evaluate each national legal order considered as a whole. A positive assessment at the global level attracts investors and foreign manpower, stimulates international exchanges and has positive effects on internal economic growth; at the same time, for the abovementioned reasons, a positive assessment at the global level acts as a proactive factor toward the search for more efficiency and for fostering the improvement of each national administrative legal environment.[22]

This means that administrative *performance* is not only considered as a value *per se*, nor it is a neutral factor at the global level, nor it is only valued for its implications upon the relationship between public administration and the citizen, under an institutional perspective. Administrative performance is rather an element, even if legal in its original nature, whose character has now taken on relevant implications under a mainly economic perspective. Nor we can say that the way information is collected, selected and evaluated for the administrative performance assessment is neutral itself, since, as highlighted by the case studies here discussed, each global institution adopts its own preferential approach, instead of taking into consideration each national administrative system as a whole.

Having shown how the outcome of the assessment on national administrative reform policy at the global level strongly depends on each institution's specific mission, should we give up looking for common principles which national administrative systems should answer to? Do global indicators have anything in common with each other? Is it possible to form a common idea concerning on what is more highly considered at the global level?

The only answer to these questions is a negative one; however, the analysis highlights some points of confluence. Something the global institutions here considered have revealed to have in

---

[22] With reference to the latter hypothesis we observe something very similar to the so called «vincolo esterno» within the Italian legal order. This is used to describe a phenomenon according to which what usually governments does not achieve because of internal pressure or lack of means, they usually manage to comply with by recalling on the European or international commitments. This mechanism is able to give start to a virtuous cycle, since a country is stimulated to improve its legal system because of other countries' improvement: can this work the same for administrative performance? For further discussions on this, see S. Cassese, *L'evoluzione recente dello Stato italiano*, on *Giorn. Dir. Amm.*, 2004, p. 673.

common, as far as priorities are concerned:as to administrative law sectors, economic public law is the one which raises more concern, both according to information purpose and to conditional mechanisms; as to policies, specific relevance is given to de-regulation and liberalization, followed by privatization, contract policies in public spending, debt and inflation control, development-oriented policies in the labour market.

Even if the assessment function at the global level has given priority to various fields of reform, it also focuses on different aspects within them; all of the global institutions taken into consideration have been concerned mainly with three policies. Particular attention has been paid to deregulation, liberalization and privatization. As a consequence, we can argue that, generally speaking, a positive assessment of national administrative efficiency has been made through the standards of the quality of regulation with specific attention on the lightening of national bureaucratic burdens,[23] as the most relevant factors taken into account by the assessment by global institutions.

This is not surprisingly if we consider that the enlisted administrative reform policies are the ones which mainly act as stimuli for the growth and the development of the global economy; accordingly, anything which is not directly instrumental to this aim has been considered as secondary.[24]

In as much as we pointed out at the beginning of this study, and the fact that globalization is proactive toward national administrative reform, we can therefore now add that, at the global level, the only administrative reforms which are of value are those which, upon a sector-oriented perspective, most stimulate globalization itself. Nevertheless a certain degree of uniform-

---

[23] About it, in terms of «concezione minimalista dello Stato», see S. Salvi, M. Salvatore e A. Zuliani, *L'amministrazione pubblica italiana nel contesto competitivo europeo*, Documento Mipa, Roma, p. 9.
[24] On the secondary relevance assigned to a series of interest, M. D'Alberti, *Poteri pubblici, mercati e globalizzazione*, il Mulino, Bologna, 2008.

ity in assessment should be properly balanced with an approach conscious of the diverse nature of each reform policy as well as of the various environments where they grow up. If, as is natural, this has led to the growing involvement of economics into the assessment decision, nevertheless, a proper appreciation of administrative reform policies cannot be developed, on the one hand, without a common criteria of principles, while, on the other, without taking into consideration the entire socioeconomic context where each study takes place.

CHAPTER VI

OUTLINE OF THE FRENCH PRACTICE OF REGULATORY IMPACT ASSESSMENT (RIA) SYSTEM PRELIMINARY TO THE LEGISLATIVE PROCESS, ONE YEAR AFTER THE ENACTMENT OF THE NEW 2008 CONSTITUTIONAL FRAMEWORK

JEAN MAÏA*

* Head of the Department "Legislation and Quality of the Norm", Secretari-at-General of the Government (SGG).

CONTENTS

I. RIA New Institutional French Framework Supports the Legislation-Making Process 169

  1. RIA Mechanism of Control is Double: Political and Jurisdictional 169

  2. RIA Process is Defined by the Government from a Concrete and Operational Point of View 172

II. Preliminary Results of the French RIA Policy Since the 2008 Constitutional Reform – Beyond Operational Difficulties, RIAS Contribute to the Reduction of Uncertainty in the Decision-Making Process and to the Promotion Of Public Debate 174

  1. From a Practical Point of View, the Scope of Impact Assessments Turns Out to be Unnecessarily Wide Due to the New Institutional Framework Defined In 2008 174

  2. Impact Assessments, Uncertainty and Public Debate: The Case of the Bill Establishing a New Organization of the Electricity Market (*Projet de Loi NOME*) 177

III. Conclusion 179

THIS paper aims to provide an empirical point of view of RIA and the importance devoted to economical analysis in that studies. For more than a year, French government implements new constitutional rules, these rules have deeply renewed RIA preparation.

French original institutional method and the resources available to carry out impact assessments must be presented first in this paper (1). Then, commentaries to this new system must be pointed out and we will end this demonstration with the methodological difficulties (2).

This paper does not intend to develop an exhaustive theory of the French RIA system but to provide some concrete elements to the discussion about the preliminary evaluation approach, its contribution to the decision-making process and the expectations in terms of law quality and effectiveness.

I. RIA NEW INSTITUTIONAL FRENCH FRAMEWORK SUPPORTS THE LEGISLATION-MAKING PROCESS

1. RIA MECHANISM OF CONTROL IS DOUBLE: POLITICAL AND JURISDICTIONAL

Regarding RIA mechanism of control, the constitutional review of 23 July, 2008, has introduced several changes to the Constitution which make France different to other OECD countries.

The French RIA process is no longer based on Circulars from the Prime Minister, but on Article 39 of the Constitution. The elaboration of a RIA for every bill is now a constitutional obligation. Article 39,[1] paragraph 3, mandates that *"the tabling of government Bills before the National Assembly or the Senate, shall comply with the conditions determined by an Institutional Act"*, namely the Institutional Act of 15 April, 2009.[2]

This constitutional obligation covers ordinary bills, finance bills and social security financing bills but it excludes constitutional reforms and legislative bills.

Impact assessments have to respond to the requirements defined within Article 8 of the Institutional Act.. These guidelines are not very different from international standards in terms of diagnostic tools, definition of objectives, options analysis and impact assessments but insist as well on the obligation of data quantification and explanation of chosen figuring methods. French and European evaluation systems share a transversal and sustainable development approach focused on the analysis of social, environmental, economic and financial aspects.

The mechanism of political control relies on the possibility given to *"the Conference of Presidents of the first House to which the bill has been referred"* to refuse to include it on the agenda if *"the rules* (concerning the impact assessment) *determined by the Institutional Act have not been complied with"*. This mechanism has been implemented for the first time in August 2008, before the National Assembly. The Conference of Presidents discussed the quality of the RIA related to the pension bill but decided not to include it on the agenda.

---

[1]   http://www.conseil-constitutionnel.fr/conseil-constitutionnel/root/bank_mm/anglais/constiution_anglais_oct2009.pdf

[2] http://www.legifrance.gouv.fr/affichTexte.do?cidTexte=JORFTEX T000020521873&fastPos=1&fastReqId=1684397550&categorieLien=cid &navigator=naturetextenavigator&modifier=LOI&fastPos=1&fastReqI d=1684397550&oldAction=rechTexte

The mechanism of jurisdictional control is applied "*in the case of disagreement between the Conference of Presidents and the Government.*" In such a case, "*the President of the relevant House or the Prime Minister may refer the matter to the Constitutional Council, which shall rule within a period of eight days*".

Two other aspects of the French RIA system must be underlined: impact assessments are first examined with bill projects by the Council of State and then by the Council of ministers and Parliament. Impacts assessments have a public feature: they are released as soon as bills have been referred to Parliament. The public nature of impact assessments contributes to strengthen parliamentary and public debates. For instance, since 2009, the National Assembly has decided to offer to visitors on its web site the possibility of commenting on the impact assessments. The Member(s) of Parliament in charge of the introduction of the bill then revise and append the comments to the report. Moreover, several impact assessments have fuelled public debates on Internet or in the press.

1. Outlining the genesis of the original new institutional framework implemented in 2008, emphasises how difficult it was to connect the preliminary evaluation approach to the decision-marking process

The connection between France and RIA has been paradoxical for some time. It cannot be denied that France was one of the first OECD countries aware that the struggle to overcome legislative excess and consequent legal instability required the implementation of impact assessment[3] – even ten years beforethe US. However, those intentions did not change habits despite a series of circulars[4] from the Prime Minister, that was not imple-

---

[3] See the following reports : "De la sécurité juridique", Council of State, 1991; "L'Etat en France – server une nation ouverte sur le monde", Jean Picq, 1994;

[4] 1995, 1998, 2003, etc.

mented. Consequently, the Council of State suggested in 2006,[5] that the only way to succeed in making impact assessments compulsory was to o require them at the highest level in the hierarchy of norms. This recommendation was considered by both the Government and Parliament in the discussions concerning the constitutional reform of 23 July, 2008. As a result, the RIA process was incorporated into the Constitution (Article 39), and established more specifically in the Institutional Act of 15 April, 2009, as a significant piece of the legislative and decision-making process,

2. RIA PROCESS IS DEFINED BY THE GOVERNMENT FROM A CONCRETE AND OPERATIONAL POINT OF VIEW

The department in charge of tabling a regulation is responsible for carrying out the impact assessments. The Secretariat-General of the Government coordinates this process at an interdepartmental level and also provides methodological support and monitors the impact assessments' quality in connection with advisers from the Prime Minister's Cabinet Office. The final document is issued by the Government, in addition to the department proposing the regulation.

The Secretariat-General of the Government intervenes at four stages during the RIA process:

- Stage 1: Drafting of the specifications chart:
  - As soon as possible, the leading department should send to the Prime Minister' Cabinet a guideline document;

---

[5] See the report « Complexité du droit et sécurité juridique »

- The drafting of the requirements follows, during a meeting between the leading department services and the SGG;
- The requirements are to draw up in an outline of the impact assessment in order to schedule it and to determine crucial points.

- Stage 2: During the drafting process, the SGG provides methodological support – based on official guidelines – to the leading department. The SGG also supervises the diffusion of the impact assessment draft to the other departments involved, collects their observations and chairs meetings at an interdepartmental level in order to reach a consensus.

- Stage 3: The SGG adapts the impact assessment taking into account the bill evolution and the observations of the involved departments.

- Stage 4: The control stage of the impact assessment:
  - Before delivering the impact assessment and the bill to the Council of State, the SGG controls their quality in coordination with the Prime Minister's staff;
  - Before the presentation of the bill to the Council of Ministers, the SGG is expected to take into account the changes proposed by the Council of State;
  - The First Chamber to which the bill is referred is responsible for the quality control of the impact assessments, this control can also occur at any time during the legislative process.

II. PRELIMINARY RESULTS OF THE FRENCH RIA POLICY SINCE THE 2008 CONSTITUTIONAL REFORM – BEYOND OPERATIONAL DIFFICULTIES, RIAS CONTRIBUTE TO THE REDUCTION OF UNCERTAINTY IN THE DECISION-MAKING PROCESS AND TO THE PROMOTION OF PUBLIC DEBATE

From 1 September, 2009, to 31 August, 2010 a few as 83 impact assessments have been referred to Parliament.

1. FROM A PRACTICAL POINT OF VIEW, THE SCOPE OF IMPACT ASSESSMENTS TURNS OUT TO BE UNNECESSARILY WIDE DUE TO THE NEW INSTITUTIONAL FRAMEWORK DEFINED IN 2008

Regarding impact assessments, France made the choice of combining economic, social and environmental approaches. The wideness of the scope required in the development of the analysis makes it difficult to keep them understandable and concise. Indeed, most of the impact assessments consist of more than 50 pages and this puts into questions their possibility to have an effective influence the decision-making process.

The impact assessments guidelines in terms of economic analysis are:

1) Macroeconomic impacts: with the effects concerning:
   a) Economic context: dynamism of economic activities, GDP, inflation level;
   b) Economic competitiveness of France: global competitiveness of French companies, trade balance, foreign economic relations, tourism industry, foreign direct investments, etc.
   c) Free market performance, consumer protection;

d) Free competition or competition imbalance;

e) Local impacts: employment areas, local attractiveness and competitiveness;

f) R&D: technological progress, new technologies, academic and applied research.

2) Microeconomic impacts on every individual or corporate body that may be concerned:

a) Impacts on companies in terms of administrative charges, taxation, investments opportunities or constraints; impacts regarding the characteristics of the company (size, sector, employees skills level); access to main inputs (working force, raw materials, energy resources); specific impacts on small businesses.

b) Impacts on individuals in terms of administrative charges, utilities, purchasing power level, information, consumer protection.

In order to improve the analysis of the new administrative duties placed on administrations, companies and individuals, the SGG has developed a specific tool dedicated to the economic section of impact assessments, named is "OSCAR". This tool aims to promote and assess these administrative duties. OSCAR relies on the standard cost model and on a methodology developed by both DGME and IGF[6] and on data collected by DGAFP, INSEE and DB.[7]

In addition to the innovations OSCAR provides, the Prime Minister has recently appointed to the SGG a Commissioner in charge of Simplification. One of his missions is to ensure that

[6] DGME : Direction générale de la modernisation de l'Etat ; IGF : Inspection générale des Finances
[7] DGFAP : Direction générale de l'administration et de la fonction publique ; INSEE : Institut national de la statistique et des études économiques ; DB : Direction du budget

new rules for corporate activities are well assessed, concerning the need of the industrial sector and small businesses.

Nevertheless, it is inevitable that each impact assessment must be adapted to the corresponding bill contingent to the political expectations and to the perceived issues of the regulation. In addition, from a practical point of view, quantifying and assessing as a whole the expected impacts appear to be unrealistic. No quantitative analysis can rely entirely on clear hypothesis or parameters. Moreover, these parameters can generate varied and heterogeneous impacts. For instance, those impacts could turn out to:

- be more or less diffuse;
- be more or less perceptible over the long-term;
- evolve in the course of time;
- be difficult to monetize;
- raise methodological and theoretical issues;
- be the consequence of various, tangled and complex systems; or
- affect differently individuals or economic areas.

In addition, collecting all the appropriate data and carrying out relevant simulations is not always easy. Indeed, Treasury services possess a significant expertise in simulations and macroeconomic models but sometimes their feedback on these endeavours is patently incomplete. Consequently, the objective of the RIA process should be to contribute to the reduction of uncertainty in the decision-making process rather than to assess economic impacts scientifically.

2.BIMPACT ASSESSMENTS, UNCERTAINTY AND PUBLIC DEBATE: THE CASE OF THE BILL ESTABLISHING A NEW ORGANIZATION OF THE ELECTRICITY MARKET (*PROJET DE LOI NOME*)

Despite the difficulties mentioned above, the RIA process should not be condemned or considered useless in relation to the decision-making process. The new institutional framework that has been launched in France in the past year has helped to streamline the parameters of public decisions.

The complex case of the bill establishing a new organization of the French electricity market illustrates the advantages and disadvantages of impact assessments. Indeed, from the economic analysis point of view, the electricity market presents itself as a complex case, which requires managing many uncertain parameters. The bill's objective is to better reconcile the principles of profit and public service in the French context, where electricity generation has a significant nuclear component. Consequently, the bill aims to adapt the economic conditions of the French electronuclear market to the prices existent in European electric wholesale markets, in order to satisfy both electricity suppliers and consumers[8]. Other difficulties arose in the production of the associated impact assessment[9]. Among them was the question of defining a precise framework for future indefinite decisions necessary, and likely to cause serious impacts.

However complex and problematic the subject may be, impact assessment is evidence of the dynamism of the new institutional framework for RIA process, and has generated interest and varied reactions, notably in the research community. For instance, the Centre of Industrial Economics of Mines ParisTech (CERNA)

---

[8] For more details, see the « Champsaur » report (April, 20009): http://lesrapports.ladocumentationfrancaise.fr/BRP/004001811/0000.pdf

[9] See : http://www.legifrance.gouv.fr/html/actualite/actualite_legislative/EI_marche_electricite.pdf

released a study in June 2010, which highlights the pros and cons of the impact assessments:

a) Advantages:
- the language used is understandable, especially for the uninformed public;
- the difficulties in reconciling the objectives set with the foreseen impacts of the reform are well explained;
- the impact assessment provides a multitude of facts and figures, some of which are not well-known; and
- the impact assessment contributes to the promotion of public debate.

b) Disadvantages (in terms of methodology):
- some assertions are scarcely supported, if at all, notably regarding legal stability and security. Indeed, it is quite difficult to foresee exhaustively the impacts of all the parameters. Moreover, so complex a system leads inevitably to numerous changes; and
- the lack of data prevents an accurate assessment of the impacts.

In addition, an environmental think tank, the European Institute for a Reasonable Handling of the Environment (IEGRE), has taken an interest in the impact assessment related to the bill regarding "NOME". The impact assessment received a mark of nearly 6/10, even considering that IEGRE lowered the mark because the "Champsaur" report that had inspired the impact assessment had been merely attached and not fully incorporated into the document. As a result, the discontinuity between the style of the "Champsaur" report and the style of the impact assessment makes the document less readable.

Also, it must be noticed that the impact assessment related to the bill "NOME" has inspired contributions of Internet users on the National Assembly web site. Those contributions have been capsulated by the rapporteur of the relevant Commission and have contributed to the debate at the outset of the bill's examination by the National Assembly.

Impact assessments are undeniably imperfect, but no one can be indifferent to them, all the more as they contribute to further the maturation process of reforms. In this regard, the issue of the public nature of impact assessments seems to be fundamental, notably because it obligates the government to carrying them out with great care.

III. CONCLUSION

To conclude, the added value of economic impact assessments lays in the opportunity they offer not only to reduce uncertainty factors for decision-makers, but also to inform citizens, thanks to the publicity of RIA, which is put into effect when the bill they accompany is submitted to Parliament.

Without a doubt, preliminary evaluation processes should never come to an end; it is imperative that they do not breakdown. Consequently, the RIA process must continuously be improved through its use as a work tool for institutions, decision-makers and citizens. From this perspective, the link between *ex ante* and *ex post* evaluations should be reinforced.

CHAPTER VII

CAN YOU TEACH AN OLD PUBLIC LAW SYSTEM NEW TRICKS? THE GREEK EXPERIENCE ON GOOD REGULATION: FROM PARODY TO TRAGEDY WITHOUT (YET) A *DEUS EX MACHINA*

BY GEORGE DELLIS*

* Assistant Professor of Public Law at the Athens' Law Faculty

CONTENTS

I. REGULATORY IMPACT ASSESSMENT MODEL: GREECE HAD
    TO GET ONE TOO 183
    1. A National Order Without a Good Regulation Tra-
        dition 183
    2. The Introduction of a "Good Regulation" Model in
        Greece 185
    3. The Main Characteristics of the Greek RIA Sys-
        tem 188

II. FROM ILLUSION TO REALITY: A DISTORTED AND MAR-
    GINALIZED REGULATORY ASSESSMENT 192
    1. Failure to Customize the RIA Tools According to
        The Greek Administrative Reality 194
    2. Failure To Familiarize Administrators And Policy
        Makers With RIA Tools 196
    3. Lack of Transparency and Failure to Link Con-
        sultation Procedures with the Use of Specific RIA
        Tools 198
    4. The Day After the Adoption of a Regulation: Ab-
        sence of a Monitoring "Culture", of Ex Post RIA
        Evaluation and of Procedures to Enforce RIA . . . 199

III. COULD JUSTICE BE THE "DEUS EX MACHINA"?: CON-
    VERTING THE BETTER REGULATION MODEL INTO, JU-
    DICIALLY REVIEWED, CONCEPTS OF PUBLIC LAW. 200
    1. The Environmental Assessment Paradigm 202
    2. Making RIA Part of Hellenic Public Law: Perspec-
        tives and Obstacles 205

I. REGULATORY IMPACT ASSESSMENT MODEL: GREECE HAD TO GET ONE TOO

1. A NATIONAL ORDER WITHOUT A GOOD REGULATION TRADITION

G REECE has a continental law system. It is a non-federal State, with a written Constitution based on the principles of parliamentarism and a rigid separation of powers.[1] The Administration is a part of the executive branch and is supervised by the Government. Greek public law has been strongly influenced by the French paradigm. Administrative law constitutes a set of rules clearly distinguished from private law, and has mainly been elaborated by the Greek Council of State, a copy of the French *Conseil d'Etat*.[2]

Due to its continental law origins, the Greek approach on the administrative model and action has been excessively "legalistic".[3] The role of public authorities is described through legal concepts and "axiological" positions, sometimes utopistic and almost al-

---

[1] Spyropoulos/Fortsakis, *Constitutional Law in Greece*, Kluwer international/Ant. Sakkoulas publishing, Athens, 2009.

[2] Spiliotopoulos, *Greek Administrative Law*, Ant. Sakkoulas publishing, Athens 2004, Spiliotopoulos/Makridimitris (eds), *L'administration publique en Grèce*, Hellenic Institute for Administrative Science, Ant. Sakkoulas publishing, Athens, 2001.

[3] It is not without importance that the Greek Parliament is composed mostly of lawyers.

ways underestimating facts and reality.[4] The Administration is supposed to be "non-discriminatory" or "good", but not "effective" nor "efficient"; the latter qualities do not constitute general principles of the internal administrative law.[5] Moreover, it is important to stress that, despite the liberal foundations of the Greek constitutional order, the dominant view on the role of the State over the society and the markets is in favour of strong interventionism. Both right-wing and left-wing governments promote a "paternalistic" concept of the State, focusing principally on the organization of the economy, this concept that has not been challenged by the Courts[6] nor by society itself,[7] at least not until very recently despite Greece's integration in the Common Market.

Unsurprisingly, Greece ignored good regulation instruments such as Regulatory Impact Assessment (RIA) until the latter were "consensually imposed" from abroad, in the context of an attempt to present Greece as –but not to transform it into– a "modern European State". Since the nation had adopted the model of a large and very interventionist administration that did not have to be effective, evaluating the effects of its action were irrelevant and not judicially controlled. The internal legal system

---

[4] For instance, according to established case law, the citizens may evoke an "acquis social" arising from the social rights provisions included in the Constitution that prohibits Parliament to pass Laws that decrease the existing level of social protection. Nevertheless, such approach seems irrelevant, if not obsolete in a period of serious financial crisis.

[5] Regarding the need for a more realistic approach on administrative law, see Shapiro, *Pragmatic Administrative Law*, Issues in Legal Scholarship 1, 1 (2005).

[6] The Courts recognise a vast discretion to the legislator and the government for defining the "economic public interest". Since it is generally allowed to restrict private economic initiatives for public interest purposes, it goes without saying that such restrictive measures are subject to a very limited judicial review.

[7] Genuine liberal politicians occupy a marginal role in Greek politics.

traditionally implemented only sector-oriented[8] and poorly elaborated forms of regulatory assessment, such as a budgetary impact report imposed by the Constitution before the adoption of cost increasing legislative measures.[9] The "explanatory reports" that must accompany all draft legislation according to art. 74.1 of the Hellenic Constitution are, on the contrary, rather empirical essays and definitely not impact assessment studies. Moreover, public consultation procedures were unknown except in specific areas, as in the case of urban planning,[10] and even then, their importance was under-evaluated.

2. THE INTRODUCTION OF A "GOOD REGULATION" MODEL IN GREECE

The discussion concerning the necessity to implement good regulation principles and a more efficient strategic planning[11]

---

[8] Such as a review on the saturation of tourist areas, on the basis of which the national Tourism Organization planned the issuance of licenses for new hotel premises.

[9] According to Art. 75.1 HC all legislative proposals that lead to additional budgetary expenses shall be accompanied by a Report from the General Accounting Office of the State that defines the exact cost of the regulatory action.

[10] Draft Urban Plans are published and open to public discussion and objections since 1923.

[11] On the importance of strategic planning, see, Berry, *Innovation in Public Management: The Adoption of Strategic Planning*, Public Administration Review 54(4):322 (1994).

was launched only after 1995,[12] and mostly after OECD's[13] report on "Regulatory Reform in Greece" in 2001,[14] that recorded the main deficiencies of the internal public structures[15] and moved on to make specific suggestions. The conditions were favourable; during this period, Europeanization of public law was trendy,[16] European Commission was focusing on RIA[17] and Greece was

---

[12] For the first steps towards the introduction of a RIA system in Greece, see Hatzis/Nalpantidou, *From Nothing to Too Much: Regulatory Reform in Greece*, Brussels: European Network for Better Regulation; ENBR Working Paper No. 13/2007,http://ssrn.com/abstract=1075963. The authors make a special reference to a report submitted by Prof. I. Spraos to the Prime Minister in 1998 (known as "Spraos Report").

[13] In 1997, the ministers at OECD endorsed the OECD Report on regulatory reform which clearly recommends governments to "introduce RIA into the development, review and reform of regulations". See, Mahon/MacBride, Standardizing and Disseminating Knowledge: The Role of the OECD in Global Governance, European Political Science Review 1(1), 83 (2009) and OECD, *The OECD Report on Regulatory Reform: Thematic Studies* (1997), *Regulatory Impact Analysis: Best Practices in OECD Countries*, (1997), *Regulatory Policies in OECD Countries: From Interventionism to Regulatory Governance* (2002), *OECD Regulatory Policy Committee. 2009. Indicators of Regulatory Management Systems*, (2009), OECD publishing, Paris.

[14] OECD, *Regulatory Reform in Greece* [OECD Reviews of Regulatory Reform] (Paris:OECD, 2001).

[15] Mainly, overregulation, ineffectiveness, oversized public sector, lack of transparency and impartiality, corruption. See also the "Regulatory Impact Analysis (RIA) Inventory" published by the Public Governance Committee of the Public Governance and Territorial Development Directorate of OECD (Paris, April 15, 2004).

[16] Among many others, see Cassese, *The Globalization of Law*, International Law and Politics 37(2):973 (2005), Della Cananea, *Beyond the State: the Europeanization and Globalization of Procedural Administrative Law*, European Public Law 9(4):563 (2003), Harlow, *Global Administrative Law: The Quest for Principles and Values*, European Journal of International Law 17(1), 187 (2006).

[17] For a more thorough analysis, see Radaelli/De Francesco, *Regulatory Quality in Europe. Concepts, Measures and Policy Processes*, Manchester: Manchester University Press 2007, Allio, *Better Regulation and Impact Assessment in the European Commission*, in Kirkpatrick/Parker (eds), *Regulatory Impact Assessment, Towards Better Regulation?* The CRC Series on Competition, Regulation and Development, Edward Elgar Publishing, Cheltenham, UK, 2007, p.72

trying to meet the requirements for Euro Zone entry. In addition, forms of impact evaluation were already introduced in the internal legal order by EU directives in two fields: First, with the liberalisation of services of general economic interest —primarily, telecommunication and energy—, together with the implementation of independent regulatory authorities, previously unknown in Greece.[18] Second, regarding environmental protection, the introduction of an Environmental Impact Study (EIS) evaluation, which is required prior to the licensing of any project subject to cause negative effects on the environment and is submitted to public consultation, constitutes the first real form of scientific-based and open-to-the-public administrative action systematically and successfully applied in Greece.[19]

After a series of ambitious but unsuccessful attempts to produce legal texts imposing good regulation tools, RIA was finally established in Greece in 2006 by a Circular published by the Prime Minister's office, entitled "Legislative Policy and the Assessment of Quality and Effectiveness of Legislation and Regulation".[20] This choice of publication format, as well as the authority implementing RIA can be seen as having a "symbolic" value: since it is not a Law or a Decree but a Circular (which is not legally binding according to Greek administrative law) and given that the text does not come from the Ministry of the Inte-

---

and the new European Commission Guidelines of 2009: http://ec.europa.eu/governance/impact/commission_ guidelines/docs/iag_2009_en.pdf.

[18] Laws 3431/2006 and 2773/1999, respectively in the contexts of telecoms and energy, imposed a consultation procedure before the adoption of all major regulatory measures on those sectors.

[19] Already introduced since Directive 85/337/EEC and Law 1650/1986 but systematically and correctly applied, under the tight control of the Hellenic Council of State, from the mid-90s. See below, under III.A.

[20] Prime Minister's Office, Circular Y190 (July 18, 2006). For a detailed presentation of the circular and the main features of the RIA model provided for by the circular, see Hatzis/Nalpantidou (2007) and Karkatsoulis, *Regulatory Impact Assessment in Greece*, (2007) www.oecd.org/ dataoecd/19/47/39795225.pdf

rior (which has the competence to supervise the Administration in general), one could see in this choice an indication that the traditional, "over-legalistic" approach of administrative actions based on concepts and assumptions coming from public law and the administrative courts, has been left behind and replaced by a new "administrative science" approach, with an emphasis on modern governance and public effectiveness.

The circular expressly refers to the EU's Inter-institutional Agreement on better law-making[21] and OECD; it was addressed to the heads of the main branches of the administration (General Secretary of the Government, Ministries, and Regional Governments) and aimed to implement a "state of the art" vision of good administration. Despite the political turnabout of 2009, the new socialist government maintained the circular in force with some minor amendments regarding the contents of the RIA studies. It also declared its commitment to promote openness in governmental action by resorting systematically to consultation procedures[22] and implementing more attentively the RIA model.[23]

3. THE MAIN CHARACTERISTICS OF THE GREEK RIA SYSTEM

The Greek RIA system according to the circular is three-fold. Firstly, it relies on unanimously recognized *principles* to improve law-making that go beyond the legality of the text and its conformity with norms of higher rank. The system focuses

---

[21] OJ 2003/C321/01, December 23, 2003.

[22] According to the 2009 circular of the new Prime Minister, Mr. Papandreou, all draft legislation shall be open to prior public consultation.

[23] New guidelines were published in 2009 (see below) with reference the Impact Assessment Guidelines of the European Commission, the Framework for Regulatory Impact Analysis (RIA) of the OECD and the International Standard Cost Model Manual of the SCM Network.

also on *de facto* proportionality (necessity, suitability and sensu stricto proportionality) of the proposed measure and on qualities that were not very highly appreciated until then, such as simplicity, efficiency and transparency. Secondly, adherence to the above principles is safeguarded through a specific *procedure* that includes, on the one hand, the drafting of a RIA Report (RIAR) and on the other hand, the active involvement of society through open consultation. Such procedure is followed mainly for the preparation of laws enacted by Parliament and, ideally, should be extended to other forms of regulation as well. Thirdly, the circular provides for *structural* improvements designed to adapt existing public authorities to the good governance era. A central watchdog has been established within the General Secretariat of the Government to supervise and coordinate the whole project: the Bureau for the Support of Good Regulation. In addition, each administrative authority involved is to establish a special Regulatory Quality Assessment Unit (RQAU) that will undertake the drafting of RIAs and the preparation of periodical RIA reports on the progress of the better regulation policy. Another innovation of structural nature was the promotion of a codification process through a Central Codification Committee,[24] entrusted with the task of instilling rationality into the chaotic and extremely oversized internal legislation.

It is worth taking a closer view of the guidelines in force (as of 2009)[25] regarding the parameters examined in the framework of the RIA Report. The Greek system opted, at least in principle, for a sophisticated Integrated Impact Assessment (IIA) methodology that aims to cover all potential effects of the regulation under review. The Report examines at first, the *sensu lato propor-*

---

[24] Already established by Law 3133/2003.

[25] (*in Greek*): www.ggk.gov.gr/wp-content/uploads/2010/02/ypodeigma_2009.doc, the 2009 Guidelines were followed by a Manual on the preparation of the RIA Report:
www.ggk.gov.gr/wp.../Egheiridio_odigion_symblirosis_ypodeigmatos.pdf

tionality of the measure in regard to its necessity and suitability. At this stage, the Report identifies and describes the problem or issue to be regulated, together with the targets of the proposed solution on the basis of quantified elements. The "do-nothing" option must be expressly examined in comparison with the reviewed measure. The *evaluation of the regulatory consequences* includes the following sectors:

a) Economy: the Report must not only identify the concerned industries, the structural effects on the market, the effects on competitiveness, the state Budget and the national economy as a whole, but also answer specific questions such as the measure's consequences for the establishment of new economic players or SMEs. According to the 2009 guidelines, economic assessment includes the evaluation of the administrative burden (red tape) induced to the business by the new regulation on the basis of a "standardized cost model" quantifying such cost.

b) Effects on society and citizens: the Report identifies the concerned social groups and quantifies those effects through referral to the existing data of the National Statistics Service (average income, living standards, etc.). Emphasis is also given to the consequences for the citizens by evaluating whether the proposed measures will improve the services already provided by the State and simplify administrative procedures.

c) Natural and cultural environment: Any expected effects on the environment must be described and if an EIS has been undertaken for projects related to the regulation under review, its findings must also be briefly presented in the Report.

d) Administration and Justice: Pursuant to the 2009 guidelines, a part of the Report is dedicated to the implied consequences of the project for the public sector (in terms of workload and efficiency) and to the administration of justice (in terms of delays).

As for the *legality* of the regulation under consideration –which is examined after the proportionality and the evaluation of the consequences- the guidelines emphasize conformity with constitutional and European provisions, including the case-law of the Court of Strasbourg. Moreover, proof has to be given that the draft regulation has followed the approved standards for law-making (regarding textual formulation) and is in coherent with pending codification procedures. The effects of the project re-garding the distribution of powers within the Greek adminis-trative model are taken into consideration as well. It should be mentioned that, in case the proposition provides for the estab-lishment of a new public structure in the form of a committee, service, unit or public body, such proposition must be accom-panied by an additional technical report on feasibility and by a positive opinion from a special intergovernmental committee.[26] The last part of the Report deals with *transparency, social cohesion and public consultation.* It refers to the specific characteristics of the consultation procedure (time frame, means of publicity and communication, number and categories of persons involved), the main findings of that procedure and includes a brief presentation of the expressed views.

---

[26] According to another soft law text: Decision of the Prime Minister Y189/18.7.2006.

II. FROM ILLUSION TO REALITY: A DISTORTED AND MARGINALIZED REGULATORY ASSESSMENT

Examined *in vitro*, the Greek model seems to be, if not flawless, at least of high quality. However, such image is idyllic and totally misleading. Almost 5 years after its introduction in the regulatory process, very little has been done towards a realistic and correct implementation of the RIA system. Despite the number of important laws passed by Parliament after 2006, only a small portion of them was accompanied by a RIAR and even in some of those cases, the assessment was turned into parody. The example of the new insolvency legislation in 2007 is revelatory:[27] the author of the relevant RIAR shamelessly considers that the legislation in question is not supposed to produce any effects on the economy or on society.

There are some good exceptions, of course, as in the case of the recently implemented "Kallikratis Plan", which radically reformed the organization of both local authorities and decentralized administrative services in 2009, and was preceded by a true RIAR.[28] The same applies for other legislative texts produced during 2010, such as "Lifelong Learning",[29] or the introduction of an "Electronic System for the Prescription of Drugs" to contend with corruption and unjust public spending.[30] Nevertheless, even in these last two cases, the absence of technical expertise in drafting RIA studies and in quantifying effects is obvious; the people that prepared the reports, probably public servants without any specific skills, found themselves in the position requiring

---

[27] The case is presented by Hatzis/Lalpantidou, op.cit., (2007).

[28] http://www.eetaa.gr/kallikratis/Ekthesi_Sinepeion_Rithmisis.pdf *(in Greek)*

[29] http://www.gsae.edu.gr/attachments/396_ekthesi_aksiologisis_30_08. pdf *(in Greek)*

[30] http://www.hellenicparliament.gr/UserFiles/c8827c35-4399-4fbb-8ea6-aebdc768f4f7/5_EKTHESH%20AXIO.pdf *(in Greek)*

them to present the pre-existent regulation and to explain the reasons why the new project has been prepared, but could not justify them through scientific arguments and data. For other important legislative projects, RIARs have been hastily prepared ignoring the methodological and scientific principles set by the abovementioned circular and guidelines. For instance, the project aiming to introduce a "fast-track" procedure for licensing major investments in Greece –in an effort to attract foreign capital and to remove burocratic obstacles- was the object of a five-page RIA Report;[31] that document contained no specific elements or data on the negative consequences of administrative overregulation, nor on the expected benefits of the proposed legislation, but more resembled the traditional "explanatory report" that has accompanied draft legislation proposed by the Government to Parliament during the last 150 years of Greek constitutional parliamentarianism. Succinctly, it was essentially "downgrading" an RIA to a simple empirical essay drafted by civil servants without the required skills to do so.[32] In brief, the Greek RIA model presents a series of serious weaknesses that may be grouped as follows.

---

[31]   http://www.investingreece.gov.gr/files/Stratigikes_ependyseis/EK-THESI.pdf (in Greek)

[32] The same criticism may be addressed to the RIA Report on the legislation for the shrinkage of the Administration through merger or abolishment of unnecessary public units: http://www.hellenicparliament.gr/UserFiles/c8827c35-4399-4fbb-8ea6aebdc768f4f7/5 EKTHESIAXIOLOGISIS.pdf (in Greek)

1. FAILURE TO CUSTOMIZE THE RIA TOOLS ACCORDING TO THE GREEK ADMINISTRATIVE REALITY

It is generally agreed that RIAs should not be undermined by a "one-size-fits-all" practice.[33] It is necessary to adapt them to the specific characteristics of the regulatory environment in which they are to be used. Even now, the Greek public authorities have not undertaken this "shaping" process. The Government seems satisfied in solely reproducing a general RIA framework as provided for by EU or OECD texts without adjusting it to national, sectorial or local specifications. This "failure to customize" reveals indifference, or even reluctance, towards the proper use of RIA tools.

For instance, one of the major problems of the Greek economy is its lack of competitiveness due to excessive red tape burdens. The Greek Administration is a champion in imposing unnecessary, overlapping and time-consuming requirements and in prolonging licensing procedures for months or even years. Because of this, the Government should give priority to the use of the appropriate RIA tools designed to deal with this specific problem, such as the Standard Cost Model (SCM), to measure the time needed to comply with administrative requirements. Although the SCM is included in the 2009 guidelines, it has never been applied systematically. Since the scope of the RIAs is too broad and too "ambitious", tending to cover all potential effects of the examined regulation, some of the most important issues of the assessment are lost in the process. As it has been noted, a more "humble" RIA model, in two phases, "with a preliminary, simple impact assessment devoted to the analysis of alternative regulatory options and an extended impact assessment of the benefits

---

[33] Kirkpatrick/Parker (eds), *Regulatory Impact Assessment, Towards Better Regulation?* The CRC Series on Competition, Regulation and Development, Edward Elgar Publishing, Cheltenham, UK, 2007

and costs of the chosen regulatory option"[34] would be more effective.

Another major weakness of the Greek RIA model is the almost total absence of technical data that can be used for the quantification of the regulatory effects and targets. For that reason, the establishment by Law 3832/2010, of a National Statistics System supervised by a council as well as an independent authority, the Hellenic Statistics Authority, both operating under the supervision of the National Parliament, constitutes a major step forward. The close cooperation of these authorities with the relevant RIA elaboration teams could radically improve the quality of the performed assessment.

Finally, it would be more realistic to not impose RIA tools before the adoption of any normative measure as it is actually provided for in the 2006 circular.[35] It would be preferable to reserve the RIA procedure only to laws[36] and normative acts of higher importance -such as Presidential Decrees, Ministerial Decisions or Regulations adopted by Independent Authorities- and only if those texts are presumed to have significant regulatory effects, on the basis of a preliminary assessment on whether a text is worth a RIA.[37]

[34] Hatzis/Nalpantidou, op.cit. (2007).

[35] Although the circular refers to all means of regulatory action, RIAR have been prepared only in case of laws passed by Parliament and of regulations prepared by independent regulators.

[36] Including legislative amendments, as provided for in the 2009 guidelines.

[37] Such solution has been adopted also by the EC Directive on Strategic Environmental Assessment (SEA), see directive n. 2001/42/EC.

2. FAILURE TO FAMILIARIZE ADMINISTRATORS AND POLICY MAKERS WITH RIA TOOLS

Apart from imposing, *in abstracto*, the use of RIA tools, it is equally crucial to develop RIA skills within the governmental machinery and, more broadly, to accustom government employees to the use of those tools. Very little has been done in this direction. The establishment of a central RIA watchdog at governmental level within the General Secretariat of the Government (GSG) was a good decision, but that body has gradually lost its, in any case, minor role. Greece needs the equivalent of the UK's former Better Regulation Task Force, as of 2006, the Better Regulation Commission[38] with powers to exercise an even more aggressive review than that of the US Office of Information and Regulatory Affairs (OIRA) and managed by officials capacitated to impose their decisions on non-cooperative ministerial officials. The Unit within the GSG must remain but has to be significantly upgraded.

Moreover, the specific RIA units already implemented at all levels of the administration concerned (ministries, independent agencies, Prefectures, some other public bodies), with a dual task, firstly to organize RIA processes within the framework of their corresponding units and secondly, to broaden the understanding of RIA tools among the personnel and the directors of their units, did not succeed in practice. In practice, these units do not exist; the existing personnel are reluctant to occupy those posts and, in any case, are totally unqualified for the task. To be more pragmatic, the drafting of proper RIA Studies cannot be achieved –at least for a transitional period of time- without the technical assistance of external experts who can educate the relevant administrative units with the additional scientific

---

[38] Jacobs, *The evolution and development of regulatory impact assessment in the UK*, in Kirkpatrick/Parker, op.cit., (2007), p.106.

knowledge required to fulfil these tasks. Greece allocates an exorbitant portion of its national budget in unnecessary services; redirecting some of this money to bring in RIA experts would be a financially solid idea.[39] These experts could also assist the Administration in performing preliminary RIA planning,[40] which is still science fiction in Greece.[41]

Another glaring weakness of the Greek RIA paradigm is the failure to combine the use of RIA tools with codification processes. The Central Codification Commission, re-established in 2003, published a manual in 2007, which totally neglected any improvements in the regulatory effort.[42] A draft of a new law was submitted to Parliament in September 2010, on "fighting over-regulation, codification and reformation of the legislation" which supposes the creation of two committees, one concerned with codification and the other with the reformation of legislation;[43] this text refers to good regulation principles but does not expressly impose the preparation of a RIAR as a prerequisite to codification or reform.

In sum, Greece has to find a way to break with the present bureaucratic inertia and needs to bring about a major culture shift in both government and administration to overcome opposition coming from both above and from below.

---

[39] Recently, the Ministry of Interior initiated a adjudication procedure to find an expert who will provide assistance for modernizing the existing RIA model in Greece.

[40] See Jacobs, *Current trends in RIA Process and methods*, in Kirkpatrick/Parker, op. cit., (2007), p.23.

[41] Except in some specific contexts, closely linked to the implementation of sectoral EU policies through administrative agencies, as in the case of energy and telecommunications. These agencies have the resources to undertake those initiatives in close cooperation with the European Commission services.

[42] By not stipulating the preparation of a RIAR in the codifying texts.

[43] It's far from being obvious why it is necessary to create two distinct collegial bodies with such similar, if not overlapping, tasks.

3. LACK OF TRANSPARENCY AND FAILURE TO LINK CONSULTATION PROCEDURES WITH THE USE OF SPECIFIC RIA TOOLS

Consultation procedures have been brought into practice in Greece during the last 10-15 years[44] and their use is in constant increase. The Government itself has made consultation the procedural keystone of its actions. Nevertheless, it is extremely doubtful whether this procedure has improved the content of the measures taken. The problem lies in the fact that, in most cases, consultation is not linked to an organized RIA process; its scope is to stress the openness and transparency of public action from a political point of view rather than improve the outcome of the regulatory action.

To achieve the latter, two conditions seem required: *First*, it is essential for the persons participating in the consultation, to have access not only to the draft measures, but also to a "technical" study, prepared by persons with adequate scientific skills in RIA and including a non-final analysis of the pros and cons of the adoption of the measures under review. Without such scientific assistance –as in the framework of environmental decision making, where consultation follows the submission of a scientific study on environmental impacts- a discussion would not contribute to improving the regulation itself, but in merely improving the image of the Government.

Second, it is important to ensure that contributions collected during consultation, are taken into consideration during the adoption of the final decision. The existing system fulfils this requirement by imposing upon the author of the RIA Report to briefly present the views expressed during consultation. The best solution would be to provide for an update of the RIA study, al-

---

[44] Dellis, *Soft law and Consultation. Two Instruments for the Improvement of Administrative Regulatory Action*, European Public Law Series, vol. XCVIII, Esperia Publications Ltd, London, 2010, p.39.

ready open to consultation, after the completion of the latter and to integrate consultations into the final report.

The main problem relies in the fact that publication of the RIA Reports is not compulsory according to the 2006 circular and the 2009 guidelines. Nevertheless, it would be more consistent with good regulatory principles to establish as a general rule a two-step RIA process and open the process to public consultation during the initial draft of the Report, as well as publishing its final version. It's worth mentioning two important improvements that were implemented in 2010. First, many Ministries started to post RIA reports on the Internet and more recently, Parliament has followed in the same practice. In a more general context, the Prime Minister imposed from 1 October, 2010, the publication of all regulatory and administrative measures on the Internet, in order to promote transparency and accountability[45].

4. THE DAY AFTER THE ADOPTION OF A REGULATION: ABSENCE OF A MONITORING "CULTURE", OF EX POST RIA EVALUATION AND OF PROCEDURES TO ENFORCE RIA

It is not without reason that the term "monitoring" cannot be exactly translated to Greek. Unsurprisingly, public authorities lack the necessary mentality and culture to periodically evaluate the results and efficiency of adopted regulatory measures. To my knowledge, none of the regulatory measures adopted after the 2006 circular have been subject to a monitoring procedure. In any case, the limited attention that is given to monitoring and *ex post* evaluation is one of the most common weaknesses of all RIA systems around the word, even those much more advanced and mature than the Hellenic one.

---

[45] http://diavgeia.gov.gr (*in Greek*).

In addition, it is premature for the Greek model to ensure a system of proper evaluation of the RIA performance. From all known performance indicators,[46] Greek RIARs may be subject to input based, content evaluation and, to some extent, to output evaluation. On the contrary, it is impossible, at this stage, to perform any outcome evaluation by measuring the effect of RIA in terms of the quality of regulatory outcomes, or an impact evaluation of the change in regulation provoked by the RIA. Poor RIA evaluation is also a result of the fact that the central watchdog has failed in assuming that task until now.

The gap due to the lack of monitoring and *ex post* evaluation of the RIA itself may be partially filled through enforcement and sanctioning procedures. This is not possible at this point, since the existing RIA model was introduced by *soft law* texts. Nevertheless, the conversion of the process into a series of binding rules is not inconceivable, compliance would be mandatory for the Administration and, to a certain extent, judicially controlled. This issue is examined in the following, last part of the present analysis.

III. COULD JUSTICE BE THE *"DEUS EX MACHINA"*?: CONVERTING THE BETTER REGULATION MODEL INTO, JUDICIALLY REVIEWED, CONCEPTS OF PUBLIC LAW.

For a country on the verge of insolvency, with a weak, badly regulated economy and an oversized, interventionist Administration, the above-mentioned, significant incompetencies in the implementation of an effective RIA model, do not constitute a

[46] Jacobs, in Kirkpatrick/Parker, op.cit (2007), p.23.

trivial problem, but a real tragedy -in the ancient Greek sense of the world- without an apparent *"katharsis"* . Therefore, it is imperative to look for the required means to redress the situation. The solution could be found in two different approaches, an administrative and political science approach on the one hand, and a public law approach on the other.

Following an *administrative science and political science approach*, solving the problems within the Greek administrative model consists of dealing with extra-legal questions such as finding the solutions to counter the absence of qualified personnel or the lack of a broader understanding of the importance of RIA, improving the questionnaires, customizing the scope of the assessment, etc. Such an approach requires a broader change in the forms and the culture of the national Administration and would be like trying to teach an old dog new tricks. This change is by all means desirable, but (a) would be very difficult to achieve, (b) would need time and (c) would have to be based on a consensus that could be overturned at any time. Without ignoring the value of the approach in question, it must be acknowledged that it risks to fall in the same trap that initially blocked the proper implementation of the RIA model in Greece: to be too ambitious, too good to be true.

This is the reason why -at least for a traditional continental law system as the Hellenic one- it seems even more important to promote also a *public law approach*, which consists in understanding good regulation and RIA through the methods and the means of legal science and in integrating them in the rules, concepts and institutions of administrative law. RIA has been unsuccessful in Greece because of the legalistic origins of the Hellenic administrative model. From this perspective, it is not incomprehensible that an institution, such as RIA, that has developed and flourished within the Anglo-American context, faces significant difficulties when transposed to the other side of the Atlantic and the English Channel.[47] Continental systems are more rigid, more formalistic and more attached to the traditional, "Kelsenic" approach of the rule of law.[48] Forms and procedures that arise from "*soft law*" –a notion that is not easily translated outside English language- and, for that reason, not considered legally binding, are by definition underestimated, if not ignored, in systems accustomed to "understand" only requirements imposed by legal norms. Instead of trying to change the whole legalistic environment, it seems to be more pragmatic to adapt to it by converting RIA into an additional legal ingredient and a prerequisite to public action which falls under the scope of the judicial control exercised by the administrative courts. For as long as RIA remains outside Greek law, outside *public* law to be more specific, its implementation will not become truly mandatory in public administration, despite its indisputable value and its recognition –by the EU, OECD and others- as a policy tool.

1. THE ENVIRONMENTAL ASSESSMENT PARADIGM

Transforming RIA into a generalised legal obligation that covers the totality of regulatory action faces a series of theoreti-

---

[47] It is interesting to compare the reception of the better regulation approach in Greece and in Cyprus, two countries with many common, historical and cultural grounds. Nevertheless, the British occupation of Cyprus made the internal administrative and legal system more familiar with Anglo-American concepts. The Cyprus' National Action Plan For Better Regulation, initiated in 2007 and updated in 2010 is much better and more efficient than the Greek one: www.mof.gov.cy/mof/mof.nsf/.../NationalActionPlanFINAL1112010. pdf,and www.mof.gov.cy /.../DMLplaisio.../DMLplaisio_gr *(in Greek)*

[48] For a recent comparative analysis on the implementation of RIA tools in Anglo-American and continental law systems, see De Francesco, *A comparative Analysis of Administrative Innovations*, EPCR conferences, 2010, stockholm.sgir.eu/.../De%20Francesco_SIGR_ Stockholm_2010.pdf and Stewart, *U.S. Administrative Law: A Model for Global Administrative Law?*, Law and Contemporary Problems 68(1), 63 (2005).

cal and legal barriers in a continental law system. To the extent that public regulation is carried out through general regulatory and legislative acts, the introduction of a mandatory RIA prior to the adoption of such acts is equivalent to the imposition of "technocratic" motivations. Yet, according to a general principle of Greek public law, normative acts do not have to examine the advisability of the measure at stake, since, in practice, they will not be judicially reviewed according to their merits. Such exemptions are more strictly respected in the context of legislative acts. Requiring Parliament to adopt normative acts only after, and on the basis of, technical studies would appear to be an attempt to impair the democratic legitimacy of that body and the traditional concept of its role as it was recognized in continental Europe after the French Revolution. Therefore, such an obligation would be found unconstitutional and, in any case, if imposed by law, it would be set aside by another, posterior law enacted by Parliament. Moreover, the courts do not, in principle, review the compliance of Parliament with the procedural rules in the context of the adoption of legislative acts (*interna corporis* exemption).

Despite these impediments, it is not inconceivable to attribute legal effects to the failure to undertake a proper RIA before the adoption of regulatory decisions, even of normative nature. It is interesting at this point to refer to the example of the Environmental Impact Assessment and how this policy has been successfully implemented in Greece. Following a specific obligation coming from an EEC directive,[49] the national Legislature established a procedure for the evaluation of the environmental risks resulting from any public or private activity entailing such risks. The procedure in question consists of the drafting of an environmental impact study (EIS) that is open to consultation prior to the concession of the administrative license (called "environmental terms") required to carry out the action under review.

---

[49] See above, note n. 19.

The EIS is a scientific document that describes the existing environmental status of the region potentially affected by the activity to be licensed, the effects of such activity to the environment and the alternative options. This procedure is repeated periodically and before the renewal of the environmental license. After a decade of hesitations and ambiguities, and under pressure from the Supreme Administrative Court (the Greek *Conseil d'Etat*), the Administration was forced to conform to the EIA procedure, relatively unknown until that time in Greek administrative law. To come to that end, the administrative judge had to raise EIA to the level of a legal requirement, to which compliance is judicially controlled. In case of violation of the relevant procedural rules, the challenged administrative license is annulled on grounds of due process.[50] Moreover, the Council of State, despite the fact that is not entitled to enter into technical and scientific issues, uses the content of the EIS as a means to review the motivation of challenged acts and to apply a "marginal" cost-advantage test on the merits.[51] According to established case law, the drafting of the EIS and its presentation for consultation by the "interested public" constitute the main institutional guaranties for the proper protection of the environment, which is a constitutional duty of all public authorities, and the appropriate tool for a judge to review whether the economic and social benefits arising from the authorized activity are balanced compared to the environmental risks provoked by that same activity. The Court extended

[50] Dellis, Antennes de téléphonie mobile. Conseil d'État hellénique. Arrêt no 1264/2005, séance plénière, in: *Annuaire International des droits de l'homme*, Volume II, Ant Sakkoulas/Bruylant ed., Athens/Brussels, 2007. 601.

[51] Council of State (Plenary Session) 613/2002: the Court applied the cost-benefit analysis, already applied by the French *Conseil d'Etat* under the name of *bilan coût-avantages*, for assessing whether the benefits for the national economy from the operation of a gold mine in the north of Greece were more significant than the environmental costs arising from the project. The Court concluded that the administration failed in implementing correctly the cost-advantage balance.

this case-law in order to include even environmental approvals granted through statutes voted by Parliament, thus indirectly requiring Parliament to scientifically justify its decisions![52]

2. MAKING RIA PART OF HELLENIC PUBLIC LAW: PERSPECTIVES AND OBSTACLES

The EIA case law could be used as an example for the imposition of similar legal obligations in the context of the RIA, if this becomes a procedural condition imposed by legal provisions and not by *soft law* texts. Such a development is not very far away— the Ministry of Interior is currently preparing a "new regulatory framework for the improvement of regulatory governance"; after assessing the existing RIA framework, a new draft Law on regulatory government will be drafted and submitted to a vote in Parliament. When (and if) this happens, the principles, tools and procedures for good regulation, including RIA instruments, will take the form of binding rules. Moreover, since August 2010, the Regulation on House Rules stipulates that (almost) any draft law submitted to Parliament shall be accompanied by a RIA Report.[53] Consequently, Greece is not very far away from a RIA binding legislation.

Yet, the task to legally impose impact assessment tools in general is much more difficult than in the field of environmental law for three reasons: *First*, at the current stage, there is not a general duty to perform RIA coming from an EU secondary legislation describing the basic features of the impact studies as in the case of directive 85/337/EEC. *Second*, RIA also –if not mainly- concerns public *norms* and not individual acts, as in the case of envi-

---

[52] Council of State (Plenary Session) 1847/2008.

[53] Art. 85.3 of the Regulation on House Rules of the Greek Parliament (OJ 139A/10.8.2010).

ronmental licenses; as it has been explained herein, continental law is not used to the need to motivate normative acts or to their judicial review on the basis of such motivation and, *a fortiori*, is reluctant to limit the decisional powers of parliaments. *Third*, unlike the EIA, in the context of which the environmental study is performed by experts outside the administrative bureaucracy at the expenses of the (more often private) entity wishing to acquire the permit for the activity under review, the RIA is, in almost all cases, an internal administrative procedure; in principle, the reports have to be completed by the personnel of the regulator and if assigned to private experts, the costs are born by the public administration and the contracting procedures are very complex and time consuming.

These difficulties could be bypassed, at least in a significant scale. Regarding regulatory normative acts that are not passed in the form of a Parliamentary Statute, but attributed to the Executive (Government, central administration, independent authority), there are not any constitutional constraints prohibiting the introduction by law of a specific, compulsory RIA procedure, prior to their adoption. Such a procedure, in the form of the EIA, should at first engage in the drafting of a regulatory impact study[54] that would include and examine the main potential effects of the measure under review to the society, the economy and the operation of the public authorities together with possible alternative solutions. This study/report should be prepared prior to all regulatory measures of any kind that are expected to produce "significant" regulatory effects and has to made public and open for consultation before the adoption of the regulatory decision. This decision should rely on the findings of the report and take into consideration the outcome of the consultation. The respect of the abovementioned RIA requirements should be judi-

---

[54] In principle, by a specialized administrative unit or an off-counsel expert.

cially controlled by the administrative courts. The courts would be invited to decide if a RIA procedure should be undertaken or not, together with the compliance with the requirements regarding the form and the "external" content of the RIA (Has the study performed the assessments required by law?, Has it been conducted by dully qualified people?, Were the alternative options properly evaluated?, publicity of the study, consultation stage, etc.). Apart from controlling the "RIA due process", the judge may also review, on the basis of a marginal test (including reasonableness and cost-benefit) of whether the adopted regulation is consistent with the major results of the RIA procedure.

Such a method of judicial control –it should be noted that regulatory normative acts (except Laws) are, directly reviewed by administrative courts in Greece as in almost all continental law systems- is expected to have several positive effects: Firstly, it will achieve the imposition of a realistic RIA in Greece, which, if not resected, could lead to the annulment of the measures that were not properly assessed. In addition, it will improve the transparency of the regulatory action and the participation of the persons subject to regulation, who will have an interest in participating in the consultation procedure and will be more active in judicially challenging poorly prepared regulations. Finally, converting RIA in a series of legal obligations will improve and clarify the role of the judge: on the one hand, the judge will be able to broaden the scope of his review towards regulatory acts; one the other hand, there will be no risk of these reviews to become abusive, to violate the separation of powers or to cause legal uncertainty, since the judge will not challenge the content of the regulatory measure based on his own experience and ideas, but on the "objective" findings of the impact study, and if the said measure obviously contradicts the study's findings.

Regarding the regulatory choices made by Parliament during the adoption of laws, the conditions are less favourable for two reasons: a) due to the lack of a Constitutional Court, laws may not be directly challenged and annulled, b) the respect of RIA "due process" could be considered as an *"interna corporis"* issue, exempted from judicial review. Even so, it must be noted that, recently, the Greek Council of State, probably influenced by its own case-law on environmental assessment, reconsidered its traditional negative position regarding the review of the advisability of legislative measures. Since the administrative courts in Greece are entitled to incidentally review the constitutionality of the laws on which a challenged administrative act relies, and this constitutionality test includes a proportionality assessment of the legislative choices that restrict rights and freedoms, if the judges demand the legislator to prove the reasons that justified his actions, such an obligation will inevitably lead to a more consistent implementation of the good regulation principles and techniques and to an indirect judicial review of the RIA Report. For instance, the Plenary Session of the Council of State was recently called on to review the constitutionality of a law prohibiting petrol stations to operate at night at their discretion.[55] Although the majority finally upheld the constitutionality of the restriction, invoking the traditional approach that "the legislator knows better how to define public interest", a strong opposition (15 out of 33 judges) considered the law unconstitutional due to the failure of the legislator to justify his actions on specific and judicially reviewed grounds. If that approach becomes dominant, RIA instruments will allow the judge to exert a more profound review of the rationality and the proportionality of legislative choices and the absence of a proper RIA will increase the chances of a law to be found unconstitutional. In a broader context, RIA will become the meeting point of economics with administrative law,[56] a rendezvous that has not still taken place in Greece.

---

[55] CoS (Plenary Session) 1585/2010.

[56] Rose-Ackerman (ed), *Economics of Administrative Law*, Cheltenham: Edward Elgar, 2007.

RIA requirements may also be imposed on the legislator through relevant supra-legislative rules. In this context, the adoption of an EU secondary legislation providing for RIA rules before the adoption of any national measure, including parliamentary statutes, with significant effects in contexts falling in the scope of the EU legal order, could fill that gap. Unfortunately, the institutions of the EU, faithful to the "Lisbon Spirit", do not seem willing to discuss a mandatory and non-consensual RIA approach, probably so as to avoid tensions with national parliaments. Another solution for Greece would be an amendment to the Constitution, expressly referring to the principles of good regulation and integrating the RIA Study into the context of the law making process of Parliament. Until then, an updated reading of the existing constitutional provisions, under the light of good regulation standards would be a positive development.[57]

Although, Greece is a country with many excesses, over-regulation included, its main problem that has caused an unseen and evolving crisis seems to be the fruit of two severe forms of administrative pathology: a) the adoption of *bad*, -in the sense of *ineffective, uninspired, "amateur", "empirical" and corrupted*- regulations and b) the total incapacity to support, overview and monitor the implementation of, even bad, policies. Those two inadequacies of the Greek public system must, to an great extent, be attributed to the absence of good regulatory instruments such as the RIA. Therefore, one of the lessons that may be taken from the Greek regulatory tragedy is that RIA tools are indispensable, not only for curing excessive regulation, but for curing even more fundamental, functional and structural weaknesses of public action.

---

[57] Public law doctrine may combine in that context, art. 74 par. 1 HC which refers to the "reasoned report" on draft legislation, Art. 75 Par. 1 and 3 HC on budgetary assessment and ministerial financial assessment for cost increasing legislative provisions and art. 82 par. 3 HC on the Economic and Social Commission which submits to Parliament a report on economic and social effects, so as to give to RIA a constitutional status, and consider that the "reasoned report" on draft legislation is not dully "reasoned" if not based on a RIA Study.

Accepting that RIA is a method to improve the quality of the existing regulatory system is, in such a context, an understatement, instead of seeking "less" or "better" regulation, in Greece we should promote rationality in regulation and eradicate anarchy and hypocrisy (two Greek words) from public management.[58] In other terms, *the Greek system needs RIA to achieve re-regulation and not necessarily de-regulation.* To succeed in this goal, it seems important to convert good regulatory principles into compulsory legal provisions and to create a judicially controlled "regulatory due process". This public law approach on RIA is crucial but not a panacea for the *"mal Grec"*; it cannot substitute other necessary conditions such as the need for experts, to impose the requested quality of the RIA Reports, or to stop the risks of regulatory capture[59]. In other terms, Justice as a *deus ex machina* is not enough; more than one God is needed.

---

[58] See the reasoning of Torriti, *Impact Assessment in the EU: a tool for Better Regulation, Less Regulation or Less Bad Regulation* ?, Journal of Risk Research, 10, (2), p. 239 (2007).

[59] The application of RIA tools inevitably increases the importance of the "expert" vis-à-vis the politician/decision maker. This could lead to a new form of regulatory capture. Specific interest groups may have access to specialists and resources which may "divert" RIA tools towards their interests and then evoke such RIA to shift the final decision according to their needs.

CHAPTER VIII

THE REVIEWABILITY OF BETTER REGULATION. WHEN *EX ANTE* EVALUATION MEETS *EX POST* JUDICIAL CONTROL

ALBERTO ALEMANNO*

* Associate Professor of Law, HEC Paris.

CONTENTS

ABSTRACT 213

I. INTRODUCTION: TRADING OPENNESS FOR LEGITIMACY . . 214

II. THE COMMISSION'S IMPACT ASSESSMENT SYSTEM (2002-
2009) 219
  1. The Genesis 219
  2. The Evolution of the IA System 220
  3. IA Guidelines and their Scope 222
  4. The Quality Control System: The On-Going Ad-
    ministrative Review 224

III. WHEN EX ANTE EVALUATION MEETS EX POST CON-
TROL 227

IV. THE LEGAL STATUS OF THE IA SYSTEM WITHIN THE
EU LEGAL ORDER 228
  1. IA System: Lack of Legally Binding Character but
    Producing Legal Effects? 229
  2. Conclusions 231

V. THE DIRECT ENCOUNTERS: IA UNDER THE JUDICIAL
LENS 232
  1. IA and Ex Post Judicial Review 232
  2. IA and Ex Post Administrative Review 234

VI. THE INDIRECT ENCOUNTERS: CHALLENGING THE LE-
GALITY OF A EU ACT THROUGH IA 236
  1. The Procedural Check 237
  2. The Substantive Check 237
  3. IA as an 'Aid to the Parties'? 239
  4. IA as an 'Aid to the Court'? 240

VII. BEYOND 'JURIDIFICATION': THE CROSS-FERTILIZATION
PATTERNS BETWEEN EX ANTE AND EX POST EVALUA-
TION OF EU ACTS 245

BIBLIOGRAPHY 249

ABSTRACT

T HIS paper aims to explore the interactions that may arise
from the European institutions' increasing reliance on
ex ante evaluation mechanisms of proposed legislation, such as
Impact Assessment (IA), and ex post judicial review of adopted
legislation. In particular, it explores what role, if any, IA analysis
might play in the judicial review of European acts. IA is the privileged ex ante evaluation tool adopted by the EU Commission
to identify the expected effects of new legislation. Yet, lacking
a legal basis, IA does not belong to the ordinary EU decision-
making process, but merely to the highly informal pre-legislative phase. However, by opening this phase to all interested
parties, IA inevitably exposes the Commission to extra scrutiny
during a stage which has historically been more informal and
'confidential'. In particular, by offering a 'legality check' of each
Commission proposal well before its adoption, both the process
and the outcome of IA may have a role to play within the ex post
review of adopted legislation. Yet this won't necessarily happen
via a 'juridification' of the IA process as such. Rather, this will
occur through a more subtle phenomenon of cross- fertilisation
between ex ante scrutiny and ex post control methodologies. After systematizing the different encounters that might occur between IA and judicial review, this paper anticipates, by relying on
a few examples, the directions taken by these cross-fertilization
patterns.

I. INTRODUCTION: TRADING OPENNESS FOR LEGITIMACY

Although most Europeans don't seem fully aware of it, the EU governs most aspects of European modern life and touches every single individual in some way. Literally: working, travelling, communicating, eating, drinking and breathing are all activities largely governed by the EU. Although empirical data are controversial, it is safe to argue that more than 60% of Member States' legislations currently into force are no longer decided in their respective capitals, but come out of the Brussels-based decision-making pipeline. The size and authority of this growing EU body of legislation inevitably raise questions about its efficacy as well as its legitimacy.

To mitigate these concerns, the EU adopted a wave of regulatory reform measures known as 'Better Regulation' (BR) and recently relabelled, in the post-Lisbon era,[1] Smart Regulation.[2] The idea is to enhance the rationality of the EU emerging regulatory state while at the same time democratising its decision-making process. Pivotal to this regulatory reform strategy is Impact Assessment, an ex ante evaluation mechanism which is systematically applied to all Commission's major initiatives since 2002. To simplify greatly, IA requires the Commission services to identify the advantages and disadvantages of possible policy options by assessing their potential impacts and issue the final

---

[1] Behind the Lisbon mandate lied a series of criticisms about the quality of the existing legislation and dissatisfaction with previous efforts to improve the Community regulatory system. See Report of the Working Group on Better Regulation (Group 2c), May 2001, p. 21

[2] Speech by José Manuel Durão Barroso President of the European Commission VIP Corner of President Barroso and Vice President Verheugen with Mr. Edmund Stoiber, Chair of the High-Level Group of Independent Stakeholders on Administrative Burdens Brussels, 18 September 2009 (http://europa.eu/rapid/press ReleasesAction.do?reference=SPEECH/09/400)

regulation only if "necessary".[3] To duly perform an IA, the lead Directorate-General of the Commission has to gather information, [4] consult interested parties [5] and, only then, apply one of the following three methods: cost-benefit analysis (CBA), cost-effectiveness analysis (CEA), or multi-criteria analysis (MCA). Under the 2003 inter-institutional agreement on Better-law making,[6] also the European Parliament and the Council are supposed to produce their own impact assessments of "substantive amendments" in order to guarantee a uniform implementation of IA along the whole regulatory life-cycle.[7]

To mitigate these concerns, the EU adopted a wave of regulatory reform measures known as 'Better Regulation' (BR) and recently re-labelled, in the post-Lisbon era,[8] Smart Regulation..[9]

The idea is to enhance the rationality of the EU emerging regulatory state while at the same time democratising its decision-making process. Pivotal to this regulatory reform strategy

[3] IA guidelines 2009, p. 4.

[4] Communication from the Commission of 11 December 2002 on the collection and use of expertise by the Commission: principles and guidelines - "Improving the knowledge base for better policies" [COM(2002) 713 final - Not published in the Official Journal].

[5] On this communication, see Obradovic and Alonso Vizcaino, n 5 above.

[6] Inter-institutional Agreement (IIA) on Better Law-Making between the European Parliament, the Council and the Commission (2003).

[7] On how to turn this commitment into practice, see the Inter-institutional Agreement on a 'Common Approach to Impact Assessment' (November 2005). Yet the definition of what constitutes a "substantive amendment" is for each institution to determine.

[8] Behind the Lisbon mandate lied a series of criticisms about the quality of the existing legislation and dissatisfaction with previous efforts to improve the Community regulatory system. See Report of the Working Group on Better Regulation (Group 2c), May 2001, p. 21

[9] Speech by José Manuel Durão Barroso President of the European Commission VIP Corner of President Barroso and Vice President Verheugen with Mr. Edmund Stoiber, Chair of the High-Level Group of Independent Stakeholders on Administrative Burdens Brussels, 18 September 2009 (http://europa.eu/rapid/press ReleasesAction.do?reference=SPEECH/09/400)

is Impact Assessment, an ex ante evaluation mechanism which is systematically applied to all Commission's major initiatives since 2002.

To simplify greatly, IA requires the Commission services to identify the advantages and disadvantages of possible policy options by assessing their potential impacts and issue the final proposed regulation only if "necessary".[10] To duly perform an IA, the lead Directorate- General of the Commission has to gather information[11] , consult interested parties[12] and, only then, apply one of the following three methods: cost-benefit analysis (CBA), cost- effectiveness analysis (CEA), or multi-criteria analysis (MCA). Under the 2003 inter- institutional agreement on Better-law making,[13] also the European Parliament and the Council are supposed to produce their own impact assessments of "substantive amendments" in order to guarantee a uniform implementation of IA along the whole regulatory life-cycle[14] .

Given its highly participatory nature, IA is an ideal policy tool capable of shaping regulatory outcomes by combining expressed preferences with rational decision-making. Indeed, the Commission defines IA as "an essential tool for producing high quality and credible policy proposals [and which] it increases the legitimacy of EU action from the point of view of stakeholders

[10] IA guidelines 2009, p. 4.

[11] Communication from the Commission of 11 December 2002 on the collection and use of expertise by the Commission: principles and guidelines - "Improving the knowledge base for better policies" [COM(2002) 713 final - Not published in the Official Journal].

[12] On this communication, see Obradovic and Alonso Vizcaino, n 5 above.

[13] Inter-institutional Agreement (IIA) on Better Law-Making between the European Parliament, the Council and the Commission (2003).

[14] On how to turn this commitment into practice, see the Inter-institutional Agreement on a 'Common Approach to Impact Assessment' (November 2005). Yet the definition of what constitutes a "substantive amendment" is for each institution to determine.

and citizens" .[15] In some way, the adoption of IA seems to suggest the Commission's readiness to promote civic omniscience in order to achieve public consensus around its regulatory policies. However, as is often the case with policy tools that inject transparency within government, there's a flip side in the institutionalisation of IA.[16] Trading more openness for increased legitimacy may indeed be a dangerous game. By opening the pre-legislative scrutiny of the work-product of the EU administrative state to all interested parties, IA inevitably exposes the Commission to extra scrutiny during a phase which has historically been more informal, 'confidential' and "in where the bureaucrats mediate and bargain among conflicting interests".[17] This is particularly so because, by requiring an ex ante scrutiny of both substantive tests (subsidiarity and proportionality) and procedural tests (public consultation) of proposed legislation, IA offers a 'legality check' of each Commission proposal well before its adoption. As a result, by allowing interest groups to monitor the EU's decision-making process from the early stages, IA is a "fire-alarm" for pressure groups affected by proposed regulation.[18] And not only for those. IA, by dictating a more informed and more inclusive method of decision-making, enable not only private parties, but also other EU institutions as well as national parliaments to learn more about the origin, rationale and evidence underlying a Commission proposal. This might be relevant today because, after the entry into force of the Lisbon Treaty, national parliaments may,

[15] IA 2009, p. 18.

[16] L. Lessig, Against Transparency – The Perils of Openness in Government, The New Republic, October 21, 2009, p. 37.

[17] Brickman, Jasanoff and Ilgen, Controlling Chemicals: The Politics of Regulation in Europe and the United States, Itaha, New York, Cornell University Press, p. 305.

[18] Radaelli, The Political Consequences of Regulatory Impact Assessment, Paper delivered to the conference Governing the Regulatory State? Comparing Strategies and Instruments, British Academy, London, 15 January 2009

via their governments, challenge EU acts' compliance with the principle of subsidiarity.[19]

It is against this backdrop that this paper examines the relationship existing between ex ante evaluation mechanisms of proposed legislation and ex post judicial review proceedings of adopted legislation. In particular, it explores which role, if any, IA analysis might play in the judicial review of European acts by European Courts. It is structured as follow: Section 1 briefly presents the genesis, evolution, and functioning of the EU impact assessment; Section 2 offers a possible taxonomy of the encounters between ex ante evaluation and ex post control; Section 3 focuses on the legal status of the EU IA system; and Sections 4 and 5 analyse the possible interactions between the IA of proposed legislation and the judicial review of adopted legislation. Finally, the last Section, after systematizing the different encounters that might occur between IA and judicial review, anticipates, by relying on a few examples, the directions taken by the cross-fertilization patterns followed by ex ante evaluation and ex post judicial control.

Before doing so, it is crucial to introduce the EU impact assessment system. The next section will.

---

[19] Article 5.3 TEU, Article 12 (b) and Article 8 of Protocol 2 on the application of the principles of subsidiarity and proportionality. Moreover, under the new Framework agreement between the European Parliament and the European Commission, the Commission recognised the principle of equal treatment of Parliament vis-à-vis the Council of Ministers and is ready to give Parliament experts access to draft documents and preparatory meetings.

II. THE COMMISSION'S IMPACT ASSESSMENT SYSTEM (2002-2009)

1. THE GENESIS

As mentioned above, IA developed in response to the growth of the EU regulatory state and was not formally established until after 2000. Following the White Paper on Governance[20] (which highlighted the need to bring an end to the increasingly fragmented framework for EU impact assessments) and the report of the Mandelkern Group on Better Regulation in 2001[21] (which recommended the development of a more rounded tool for assessing the social, economic and environmental impact of proposed regulations), the Commission announced the Better Regulation Action Plan in June 2002.[22] This gave rise to the first guidelines on impact assessment in order "to integrate, reinforce, streamline and replace all existing separate impact assessment mechanisms for Commission proposals".[23] These guidelines, which have been recently redrafted, represent as of today the only textual basis sanctioning the Commission's reliance on regulatory impact assessment.[24]

---

[20] White Paper on European Governance, COM(2001) 428 final.

[21] The final Mandelkern report on Better Regulation was finalised in February 2001 and published on 13 November 2001.

[22] Commission Communication, Action plan 'Simplifying and improving the regulatory environment', COM(2002) 278 final

[23] IA 2002, n 8 above, 3. The Commission issued Impact Assessment Guidelines in 2003, revised them in 2005, updated them in 2006, before they were replaced by new ones in 2009.

[24] European Commission, Impact Assessment Guidelines, SEC(2009) 92. The new guidelines contain an interesting Part III: Annexes to Impact Assessment Guidelines, which finally provides a more detailed methodological guidance to the Commission services than in the past.

IA has been defined as "the process of systematic analysis of the likely impacts of intervention by public authorities"[25] and "involves building on and developing the practices that already accompany the process of policy development by deepening the analysis and formalising the results in an autonomous report".[26]

The main declared goal of IA is to improve the quality and coherence of the policy development process by ensuring that all Commission initiatives be based on sound analysis supported by the best data available.[27]

2. THE EVOLUTION OF THE IA SYSTEM

Although the EU IA system has developed "after examining established procedures in Member States and other OECD countries",[28] it presents its own specificity in terms of its scope of application and focus. Thus, for instance, while most countries apply IAs exclusively to acts of legislative nature, the Commission's system boasts a broader coverage, extending also to non-legislative proposals, such as Communications, expenditures programmes and negotiating guidelines for international agreements. Moreover, whereas most countries privilege the economic component of IA while conducting their analysis, by focusing mainly on the costs of the new regulation, the Commission's system favours a more balanced approach integrating the features of regulatory impact assessment, sustainable impact assessment and other types of ex ante policy evaluations, such as cost-benefit analysis (CBA), cost-effectiveness analysis (CEA), and multi-cri-

---

[25] *Ibid.*

[26] Communication from the Commission 'Better Regulation for Growth and Jobs in the European Union', COM(2005) 97, 4 (hereinafter "IA 2005").

[27] IA 2009, p. 6.

[28] Commission report on Impact Assessment: "Next steps - In support of competitiveness and sustainable development" SEC(2004) 1377.

teria analysis (MCA) .[29] In particular, the European Commission relies, since 2002, on an ambitious Integrated Impact Assessment model as a tool for improving the quality and coherence of its policy development process.[30] One of the few constant features is the Commission's insistence on the application of an integrated approach covering the economic, social and environmental dimensions comprehensively.[31]

Contrary to what it might appear, IA is "an aid to decision-making, not a substitute for political judgement" [32] and it runs in parallel with and feed the development of the Commission proposal. In particular, IA is promoted by the Commission not only as a tool aimed at gathering information upon which it can rely upon in order to improve regulatory rationality, but also as a way to disseminate information, to enhance legitimacy and acceptance of measures and, ideally, to provide a basis of control for the sanctioning of agents in the conduct of their activities.[33]

---

[29] Wiener J. & Alemanno A., Comparing Regulatory Oversight Bodies across the Atlantic: US OMB/OIRA and the EU IAB, in Susan Rose-Ackerman and Peter L. Lindseth (eds), Comparative Administrative Law, Yale University Press, 2010.

[30] Communication from the Commission on Impact Assessment, COM(2002) 276 final (hereinafter "IA 2002"). For an overall evaluation of the Better Regulation initiative from a US perspective, see Wiener, Better regulation in Europe, (2006) 56 *Current Legal Problems*, 447-518.

[31] This is the case since the issuance of IA 2002, p. 2.

[32] Ibidem, at 3. See also IA Guidelines 2009, p. 4.

[33] For an analysis of the current EU IA system under the perspective of the principal-agent theory, see Crowe G. (2005), Tools for the control of political and administrative agents: impact assessment and administrative governance in the European Union. In Hoffman H.C.H. and Turk A.H., EU Administrative Governance, Edward Elgar Publishing.

As "it is not possible or necessary to write a formal IA report in all cases", today a formal IA is only required for items on the Commission's Legislative Work Programme (CLWP). [34] However, the Commission may, on a case-by-case basis, decide to carry out an impact assessment of a proposal which does not appear on the CLWP [35] . Under the Commission guidelines (which are addressed to the Commission staff in charge of preparing policy proposals), IAs are carried out by the relevant Directorates-General (DG) which, under the current guidelines, rely on dedicated units ('IA support units').

Under the current guidelines, IA is structured upon the following six key steps: identification of the problem, identification of the objectives, identification of the policy options, identification of the likely economic, social and environmental impacts, comparison of the different options in the light of their respective impact and future monitoring and evaluation.[36]

As clearly emerges from this list, the EU IA model presents a complex exercise, aimed at predicting all possible consequences which may ensue from the enactment of a new regulation "whose complexity goes probably beyond that of any other impact assessment model implemented worldwide".[37]

The findings which emerge from the work undertaken for the impact assessment are presented in the form of an IA re-

---

[34] Under the Commission's rules of procedure (Art 2), the Commission defines annual priorities and adopts a work programme for each year. This programme sets out major political priorities and identifies legislative initiatives, executive and other acts that the Commission intends to adopt for the realisation of these priorities. The President presents the Commission work programme to the Parliament and the Council. See IA 2009, p. 7-8.

[35] IA 2009, p. 6.

[36] IA 2009, p. 4-5 (see table at page 5).

[37] Renda, Impact Assessment in the EU: The State of the Art and the Art of the State (CEPS Paperbacks, 2006), 55.

port. The report must specify which analytical method has been used to assess and compare the impacts (e.g. cost-benefit analysis, multi-criteria analysis, or another method). The draft IA report must be transmitted to the Impact Assessment Board (IAB)[38] at least 8 weeks before the launch of the inter-service consultation (ISC) in order to have a discussion with the Board's members, and possibly have the time to take into account their opinion. If the responsible Commissioner concludes from the IA that action is necessary,[39] a corresponding proposal will be finalised and put into ISC, together with the IA report and the IAB opinion, before finally is transmitted to the College of Commissioners for its final adoption. The IA report is then sent, after the adoption of the proposal, to the other institutions along with that proposal and is finally made available on the Europa website. To date, the Commission services have carried out more than 400 IAs.[40]

---

[38] The IAB's primary role is to oversee the quality of the IAs produced by the Directorates-General (DGs) when the latter propose new policies. The IAB is a five-member board made up of representatives from DG Enterprise and Industry, DG Environment, DG Employment, Social Affairs and Equal Opportunities, DG Economic and Financial Affairs and chaired by the Deputy Secretary-General. For an initial analysis of the IAB, see Alemanno, Alberto (2008). *Quis Custodet Custodes* dans le cadre de l'initiative Mieux Légiférer? Une analyse des mécanismes de surveillance règlementaire au sein de la Commission et la création du Comité d'évaluation des études d'impact, Revue du droit de l'Union européenne 1, 43-86.

[39] An IA report should be produced even when the Commission won't proceed with a proposal.

[40] For a list of IAs completed and planned, see http://ec.europa.eu/governance/impact/practice_en.htm. Several scholars have undertaken tentative assessments of the first IAs carried out by the Commission, see, *inter alia*, the very recent Cecot, Hahn, Renda, 'A Statistical Analysis of the Quality of Impact Assessment in the European Union', (AEI-Brookings Joint Center), May 2007.

4. THE QUALITY CONTROL SYSTEM: THE ON-GOING AD-MINISTRATIVE REVIEW

Since the launch of the IA procedure in 2002, it has been established an articulated regulatory review system within the Commission, aimed at supervising the quality of IAs performed by the Commission services. This consists of an internal, non-institutionally-independent four- level structure. The first level implies the involvement of a central IA unit, existing within each Commission DG, which controls the operational units when they prepare draft IAs. The second level of scrutiny is provided by the Commission Secretariat General[41] ('up-stream' quality control), which offers guidance and quality control on draft IAs, prepared by the relevant DGs. The third level features the intervention of the IAB, which delivers an opinion on the quality of the draft IA report with respect the IA Guidelines before the launch of the ISC. Finally, all DGs, together with the Secretariat-General ('down-stream' quality control), [42] control IA reports through the IASG,[43] which accompany the elaboration of most IAs, and also through the ISC before the underlying initiatives may reach the political level.

After having passed through all these stages of review, the final IA report, which has the status of a Commission Staff Working Document, is transmitted, together with the draft proposal, to the College of Commissioners. However, should the IA report not to be found satisfactory, the Secretariat-General or any other

---

[41] On the evolving role of the Commission Secretariat General, see D. Curtin, Executive Power of the European Union, Oxford 2009, p. 114-16.

[42] See IA 2009, pp. 7-8.

[43] Since the 2005 Guidelines, an Impact Assessment Steering Group is compulsory for all proposals of a cross- cutting nature, provides specialised inputs and brings a wider perspective to the IA process. It requires the participation of the Secretary-General, notably of its Strategic Planning and Programming Unit and excludes any input from outside of the Commission's services. See IA Guidelines 2009, p. 8.

DG may issue a suspended or unfavourable opinion at the ISC stage.[44] Ultimately, it is only if the Commission services which take part in the ISC issue a favourable opinion that the proposal will be transmitted to the College of Commissioners for a final decision.[45]

This shows how the exercise of regulatory oversight is performed by a multitude of institutional actors and takes place, in accordance with the Commission guidelines, both at up- stream and down-stream levels of the process of drafting IA reports.

The establishment of the IAB has not put an end to this heterogeneous oversight mechanism.

Unlike its US counterpart, the Office of Information and Regulatory Affairs (OIRA), which may address 'return letters' to the Federal agencies,[46] the IAB has not been entrusted with the power of a veto over IAs carried out by the departments of the Commission[47] . This choice has been perceived as weakening the effectiveness of the regulatory review performed by the IAB, which in turn cannot be considered to be the Commission's final regulatory 'watchdog'. Yet, although regrettable, this choice seems to be an inevitability, given that it has been made within the framework of the present European institutional architecture. This is because conferring upon the IAB a 'return letter' power might run against the principle of collegiality, which governs the functioning and the operation of the Commission.[48]

---

[44] *Ibid.*

[45] *Ibid.*

[46] Executive Order 12866 issued by President Clinton on September 30, 1993.

[47] J.B. Wiener and A. Alemanno, Comparing Regulatory Oversight Bodies Across the Atlantic: The Office of Information and Regulatory Affairs in the US and the Impact Assessment Board in the EU, Susan Rose- Ackerman & Peter Lindseth (eds.), Comparative Admnistrative Law, Edward Elgar, 2010.

[48] Although this principle was originally laid down in the first paragraph of Article 163 of the EC Treaty (after amendment, the second paragraph of Article 219 EC and, finally Article 250 TFEU) and is foreseen in Article 1 of

Indeed, this principle not only requires "the equal participation of the Commissioners in the adoption of decisions", but it also implies that these "decisions should be the subject of collective deliberation".[49] The rationale behind this principle is that all the members of the College of Commissioners should ultimately bear collective responsibility at the political level for the Commission's decisions.[50]

Despite these limitations, IAB opinions may produce some relevant, though indirect, effects on the outcome of the quality control process. For instance, the Secretariat-General, in taking a position within the context of the formal ISC, may block an initiative if the IAB's opinion has not been taken into account by the DG which authored the IA. As seen above, this may occur to the extent the Secretariat-General (unlike the IAB) may hold and exercise its power of veto.[51] Similarly, also private parties may try to rely on IAB's opinion when challenging the legality of a EU act whose IA report departed from that opinion.

---

the Commission Rules of Procedure (OJ 1993 L 230, p. 15), it has been fully developed by the case law of the Court of Justice. See, e.g., Case C-191/95 Commission v Germany [1998] ECR I-5449, paras 48 to 50. For an overview of the principle of collegiality, see Mistò, 'La collégialité de la Commission européenne', (2003) Revue du Droit de l'Union européenne, 189 ss.

[49] Case C-198/97, Commission v Federal Republic of Germany, [1999] ECR 3257, para 19.

[50] *Ibid.*

[51] If the IA report subject to review should not reach a satisfactory level of quality, the Secretariat-General may issue a suspended or unfavourable opinion. See IA 2006, n 22 above, 15. See on this point Alemanno, Alberto (2008). *Quis Custodet Custodes* dans le cadre de l'initiative Mieux Légiférer? Une analyse des mécanismes de surveillance règlementaire au sein de la Commission et la création du Comité d'évaluation des études d'impact, in ex post review. It is in the light of the above that the next section will attempt to answer the following questions: is the Commission (and the other institutions) legally required to perform an IA on proposed legislation? Should the Commission ensure that its proposals be based on IA? In the affirmative, would a rational relationship between adopted proposal and IA be sufficient? What, if any, are the legal consequences which flow from a departure from the analysis contained in IA?

In the light of the above, it is time to analyse the possible interactions between the IA of proposed legislation and the judicial review of adopted legislation.

III. WHEN EX ANTE EVALUATION MEETS EX POST CONTROL

When exploring which role, if any, IA might play in the Courts' judicial scrutiny of the legality of European acts, one must wonder *in abstracto* how these two different stages of the regulatory process may enter into contact. It is submitted that the possible encounters between IA results and ex post review may be envisaged in the following two main scenarios:

1) A first situation may occur should an IA report be challenged directly before Courts, for alleged breach of the relevant guidelines and procedures (so-called direct encounter).
2) A second situation may arise when an IA report is invoked in order to challenge the validity of the EU final act, either within the context of an Article 263 TFEU or 267 TFEU procedures (so-called indirect encounter).

Before examining in more details these two scenarios, it is critical to determine the legal status of the IA in the EU legal order. To gain relevance in a judicial setting, the system of IA is required, at least in principle, to be mandated by the law and, only in these circumstances, it might be productive of legal effects. This would seem to be a prerequisite for IA's relevance

IV. THE LEGAL STATUS OF THE IA SYSTEM WITH-IN THE EU LEGAL ORDER

To determine the legal status of the IA system one needs first to verify the legal nature of the acts introducing it into the EU legal order. Until now, both its introduction and implementation into the EU decision-making process rest entirely on 'atypical acts' (legal sources other than those provided for by the Treaty), such as communications, guidelines, inter-institutional agreements, which – at least in principle – produce no legally binding effects. However, these acts fall within the broader category of 'soft law' acts, which have been defined as "rules of conduct which, in principle, have no legally binding force but nevertheless may have practical effects".[52] Although these instruments are not contemplated by the Treaties, they have long been used in the EU legal order.[53] They tend to be opposed to the category of 'hard law' instruments, which regroups in turn those acts with legally binding character.

By underlying their 'soft law' status, the IA Guidelines deny that the objective pursued by the IA system is to establish procedural rights, the respect of which could be subject to judicial scrutiny. Thus, for instance, the Commission, after stressing that "IA is a key element in the development of Commission proposals, and the College of Commissioners will take the IA report into account when taking its decisions", it denies that IA may "replace decision-making – the adoption of a policy proposal is

---

[52] F. Snyder, New Directions in European Community Law, London Weidenfeld and Nicolson, 1990.

[53] For an overview on EU soft law, see the classic work by F. Snyder, 'Soft law and the institutional practice in the European Community', in S. Martin (ed), The Construction of Europe, Essays in Honour of Emile Noël (1994), pp. 197-225 and Lefevre S., 'Interpretative communications and the implementation of Community law at national level', European Law Review, 29 (2004), 808-822.

always a political decision that is made only by the College".[54] Consequently, an individual or a EU institution which should not be happy with the way in which an IA has been performed by the Commission services would not seem to be entitled to apply for judicial review in order to obtain a scrutiny over the relevant final EU action.

Though prima facie surprising, the introduction of the IA Guidelines through administrative guidelines instead of legislative acts is not unusual when compared with other experiences of regulatory reform.[55] Indeed, in most OECD countries, impact assessment and consultation duties, though also emanating from a high executive level, have occurred through the adoption of soft law documents.

1. IA SYSTEM: LACK OF LEGALLY BINDING CHARACTER BUT PRODUCING LEGAL EFFECTS?

In any event, the fact that IA procedures have been introduced within the legal order through guidelines and communications, which are atypical instruments not even mentioned in Article 288 TFEU, does not necessarily mean that cannot produce legal effects. Indeed, the case law of the European Courts shows that not only recommendations [56] but also other 'soft law' instruments may produce legal effects. With this in mind, one might wonder to what extent the IA Guidelines may produce legal effects which are directly enforceable before the EU courts.

A look at the case-law shows that the question of the application and enforcement of self- imposed rules has arisen firstly in

---

[54] IA Guidelines 2009, p. 4.

[55] Rowe, supra, p. 475; F. De Francesco, Combining innovation and administrative attributes: The typologies of rulemaking (on file with the author), p. 12-14.

[56] Case C-322/88, Grimaldi [1989] ECR 4407.

the area of staff cases, in relation to internal rules sketched out by the institutions. It is in this area that a self-binding effect for self-imposed rules has been recognised, on the basis not solely of the principles of equal treatment and legal certainty but also on the basis of other principles of law, such as *patere legem quam ipse fecisti*, legitimate expectations and essential procedural require-ments. In relation to this very last principle, there are a couple of judgments which recognise that self-imposed rules may have a self-binding effect upon the Commission .[57] This principle seem to have been extended, beyond the area of staff law, into other fields. In particular, the principle of equal treatment has been increasingly used to establish a finding that there is a self-binding effect. One of the first examples of this trend is *Thyssen v Commission*, in the ECSC area, where the court implicitly acknowledged that the administration may be bound by its own practices on the basis of the principle of equality (although in this case the court went on to hold that the situations before it were incomparable).[58] A more illustrative example of such a spill-over into other areas of law is the *Hüls v Commission* case, in which the Court of First Instance (today General Court) concluded that when the Commission imposes procedural rules on itself - in this case a procedure for providing access to the files in competition cases contained in the 12th Report on Competition Policy - it "may not depart from rules which it has thus imposed itself".[59] The Court in this case seems to have reached this conclusion by relying on the principle of equal treatment, rather than on that of a breach of an essential procedural requirement.

It should also be noted that the recognition of such self-bind-ing effects depends on the nature of the rules at issue: the more

---

[57] Case 282/81, Ragusa v Commission [1983] ECR 1245 and case 263/83, Turner v Commission [1985] ECR 893.

[58] Case 188/82, Thyssen v Commission [1983] ECR 3721.

[59] Case T-9/89 Hüls v Commission [1992] ECR II-499.

absolute and clear their formulation, the more scope there is for a finding that these rules have a self-binding effect.[60] Thus, the court has held that:

> "[T]he Community institutions may lay down for themselves guidelines for the exercise of their discretionary powers by way of measures not provided for in Article 249 EC, in particular by communications, provided that they contain directions on the approach to be followed by the Community institutions and do not depart from the Treaty rules. In such circumstances, the Community judicature ascertains, applying the principle of equal treatment, whether the disputed measure is consistent with the guidelines that the institutions have laid down for themselves by adopting and publishing such communications".[61]

2. CONCLUSIONS

To sum up, EU courts seem increasingly willing to consider the EU institutions to be under a duty to act in a consistent and non-arbitrary manner, which entails a duty to apply the rules that it has established for itself. However, as our analysis has shown, while it is true that a self-binding effect for self-imposed rules seems to have gradually found its way within the EU legal order, it remains to be seen to what extent, and on which basis, this case-law may be extended to the IA soft law documents. On this

---

[60] Case C-156/98 Germany v Commission [2000] ECR I-6857.

[61] See Case T-13/99 Pfizer Animal Health v. Council, [2002] ECR II-3305, para 119. See also, to that effect, Case T-7/89 Hercules Chemicals v Commission [1991] ECR II-1711, para 53; Case T-149/95 Ducros v Commission [1997] ECR II-2031, para 61; and Case T-214/95 Vlaams Gewest v Commission [1998] ECR II- 717, paras 79 and 89.

point, it might be observed that, unlike most of the self-imposed rules which were at issue in the abovementioned judgments (a memorandum from the Director-General, an internal guide, etc), the IA Guidelines appear to enjoy a greater institutional and political weight. In particular, the IA guidelines find their origins in resolutions and policy statements of the European Council and contribute to the implementation of express Commission policies .[62] Moreover, as shown above, the implementation of the IA system by the Commission services is susceptible to be administratively enforced within the Commission hierarchy via the quality control mechanisms.

V. THE DIRECT ENCOUNTERS: IA UNDER THE JUDICIAL LENS

1. IA AND EX POST JUDICIAL REVIEW

The most obvious, and perhaps violent, encounter between ex ante analysis and judicial review may occur when the legality of the former is challenged under the latter. Thus, one may envisage that an IA report be challenged directly before Courts, for alleged breach of the relevant guidelines and procedures. Under such a scenario, the plaintiff may claim the absence of IA or claim that the analysis conducted under IA are vitiated by a breach of the relevant guidelines and procedures. One may even claim that the IA didn't take into account the IAB report.[63] Yet

---

[62] See, e.g., Resolutions of Göteborg and Laeken European Councils; the Better Regulation Action Plan COM(2002) 278 and the Action plan to improve communicating Europe by the Commission, SEC(2005)985.

[63] This situation doesn't seem very likely to occur to the extent the IA Reports, like the Commission proposals, are not published before the publication of the IAB Report. This would indeed make it difficult to challenge the

this direct encounter is quite unlikely to occur. Being a mere 'preliminary act', an IA report, although stemming from a EU institution enshrined in Article 263 TFEU, is not liable to produce legal effects and, as a result, it would be considered by the courts as a non- reviewable act (*acte ne faisant pas grief*).[64] Moreover, regardless of its nature, the courts would struggle in any event to review the correctness of the analysis conducted under the IA methodologies, to the extent that the latter are not readily usable benchmarks.[65] Therefore any direct action against an IA would be likely to be declared inadmissible by the courts. However, insofar as the Commission's non-compliance with the IA Guidelines may be considered a case of maladministration, any departure from the IA guidelines may be brought before the European Ombudsman.[66] This in principle should extend to any IA-related breach of the Inter-institutional Agreement for Better Law Making and may lead other institutions' actions, such as those of the Council and the Parliament, to be considered as instances of maladministration.

---

divergence between the original Commission Proposal/IA Report (which will never be published) and the IAB Report.

[64] On this category of acts, see Schermers and Waelbroeck, Judicial Protection in the European Union, (Kluwer, 2003), 348-355.

[65] Largely due to their methodological vagueness, the IA tools and procedures (as laid down in the Guidelines) do not seem easily applicable for the purposes of verifying whether the Commission services have applied them correctly. Thus, for instance, how could the courts check whether the IA performed conforms to the principle of proportionate analysis? This principle has been introduced by the 2005 IA Guidelines, and must not be mistaken for the general principle of proportionality. Its application requires that depending on the significance of the EU action some aspects of the analysis be more or less developed. In other words, the more significant an action is likely to be, the greater the effort of quantification and monetisation that will generally be expected.

[66] The European Ombudsman, Decision 948/2004/OV of 4 May 2005.

A less violent encounter between IA and ex post control might take place before the European Ombudsman. Under Article 229 TFEU, the Ombudsman may investigate complaints from EU citizens in instances of maladministration, "with the exception of the Court of Justice of the European Union acting in its judicial role". According to AG Geelhoed, "[T]he main purpose of the procedure before the Ombudsman is to give citizens the possibility of seeking satisfaction in cases where judicial proceedings are not an option or would not produce an appropriate result".[67] Indeed, the status of the Ombudsman enables him "to combine the instruments of parliamentary scrutiny and judicial control in an original way".[68]

Therefore, as previously mentioned, should the Commission's non-compliance with the IA guidelines be considered to be a case of maladministration, any departure from these procedural requirements may be brought before the Ombudsman. Thus, for instance, following a complaint by the European Citizen Action Service concerning the alleged failure of the Commission to inform and consult NGOs on the future of Structural Funds, the Ombudsman held that it "[...] would [...] regard failure to comply with procedures and principles set out in the Communication on minimum standards for consultation as maladministration".[69] Therefore, although the Ombudsman found no instance of maladministration in that particular case,[70] the Ombudsman's

---

[67] Opinion of AG Geelhoed delivered on 3 July 2003, case C-234/02 P, European Ombudsman v Frank Lamberts, para 65.

[68] P. Magnette, Between Parliamentary Control and the Rule of Law : the Political Role of the Ombudsman in the European Union, Journal of European Public Policy, 10/05, p. 677-94, p. 690.

[69] Ombudsman decision, 948/2004/OV of 4 May 2005, para 3.8.

[70] It stated that "on the basis of the available information [...] the Commission appears to have organised a genuine consultation process with regard to

office unequivocally asserted its competence over any departure from the minimum standards for consultation.[71] Moreover, since the complainant also questioned whether these standards were sufficiently clear, the Ombudsman pointed out that, without excluding the possibility that these could be expressly more clearly, the review which he carried out demonstrated that they may applied without difficulty to verify whether the Commission has complied with them.[72]

Although there are no cases, at least to our knowledge, in which a departure from the IA guidelines has been brought to the Ombudsman as a possible instance of maladministration, it is submitted that this allegation, by analogy, would hardly fall outside the competence of the Ombudsman.

The existence of such an ex post administrative review is relevant and may produce practical effects. Indeed, an Ombudsman decision qualifying as an instance of maladministration the departure from the IA Guidelines may facilitate the plaintiff's attempts to obtain damages from the European Courts.[73]

Thus far, the only complaints founded upon alleged violations of the IA guidelines have instead been brought to the attention of the Commission's Secretariat-General and have not led to any formal decision.[74]

---

its cohesion policy". See Ombudsman decision, 948/2004/OV of 4 May 2005, para 3.9.

[71] Commission communication 'General principles and minimum standards for consultation of interested parties by the Commission' COM(2002)704. On this initiative and more in general, on the formalisation of civil group's involvement in EU policy conception, see Obradovic and Alonso Vizcaino, 'Good Governance Requirements concerning the Participation of Interest Groups in EU Consultation', (2006) Common Market Law Review 43, 1049-1085 (2006).

[72] Ombudsman Decision, supra, para 3.16-17.

[73] Article 340 TFEU. See Case T-209/00, Frank Lamberts v European Ombudsman, [2002], paras 58-59

[74] Phone interview with an official working at the Secretariat-General.

VI. THE INDIRECT ENCOUNTERS: CHALLENGING THE LEGALITY OF A EU ACT THROUGH IA

A less immediate, yet more likely, encounter between IA and judicial review may arise when the IA report is invoked before Courts in a validity challenge against the final EU act. This might occur either within the context of an Article 263 TFEU or 267 TFEU procedures. In particular, a Member state, an institution, or even an individual (provided that that individual satisfies the *locus standi* conditions in the case of a direct action) [75] could challenge the legality of a EU act for breach of the IA procedure. This breach might be procedural or substantive. To be successful in the former case, the plaintiff should show that:

1. IA amounts to an "essential procedural requirement", within the meaning of Article 263.2 TFEU, and
2. that the Commission, when performing (or non performing) IA, has infringed such a requirement.

In the latter case, instead, the plaintiff may challenge the legality of a EU act by claiming that it conflicts with the IA analysis conducted with respect to the principles of conferral, proportionality and subsidiarity. Thus, for instance, policy op-

---

[75] The Lisbon Treaty does not only extend the preliminary ruling procedure to the validity (and interpretation) of acts emanating from all EU "bodies, offices or agencies", but it also eases the conditions for the admissibility of actions brought by individuals against EU acts. Under Article 263 (4) (former Article 230.4), "any natural or legal person may [...] institute proceedings ... against a regulatory act which is of direct concern to them and does not entail implementing measures". Hence, having the requirement for individual concerned being dropped for challenges directed against 'regulatory acts", the *Plaumann* test will survive only with reference to "non- regulatory acts". It remains to be seen how the General Court and the ECJ will interpret this notion (all non- legislative acts or also some legislative acts?). Regardless of the interpretation which will finally be given by the EU judiciary, Article 263.4 is likely to improve individuals' access to justice within the EU. See, Mancinus, When the European judicial cathedral loses the pillars and opens the gates (?), www.adjudicatingeurope.eu

tion b under IA didn't pass muster in any of those tests, but was incorporated into the final act. Is that act legal? Can (or should) IA offer a valid benchmark for the Court's scrutiny of the legality of the final act?

1. THE PROCEDURAL CHECK

It is clear that to be successful in a procedural check scenario, the plaintiff will have to prove that IA represents a binding step in the EU decision-making process, whose omission, or incorrect application, might affect the legality of the final act. As illustrated above, the introduction of the IA system into the European legal order through 'soft law' acts renders this a particularly difficult task. However, given the case-law recognising legal effects of self- imposed rules, it cannot be totally excluded that the courts could hold that IA is an "essential procedural requirement" to which the Commission must abide by during the drafting stage of its initiatives. Should the Court take this path, it is likely that the plaintiffs could easily prove that the IA Guidelines are not always respected by the Commission.[76]

2. THE SUBSTANTIVE CHECK

When conducting an IA the Commission is inter alia expected to verify ex ante whether its policy proposals conform to the principles of conferral, proportionality and subsidiarity. Hence, to want extent European courts, when called upon to review the validity of the final act, may or should rely on these previ-

---

[76] As it stems from the IAB annual report, one of the most common problems in the performance of IA reports by the Commission services is the lack of identification of different policy options. See IAB Annual Report, 2009.

ous analyses in order to determine whether the challenged act complies with these principles? Thus, for instance, what is the relationship between the ex ante proportionality test exercised by the Commission within IA on a proposed regulation and the ex post proportionality test under judicial review of the adopted regulation? How this ex ante 'pre-legality check' and the ex post 'legality checks' on the same principle should, if at all, interact?

Although the Courts have been able to assess – at least until now – the compliance with these principles without necessitating any analysis at the drafting stage of the proposal, the current practice of carrying out an IA for all major Commission initiatives might lead the Courts to refer to such previous evaluations before reaching their conclusions. This might occur as a result of the Courts acting *sua sponte* or upon request of the parties. For instance, when assessing whether a final measure falls within the competence of the EU, the Court might look at how this question has previously been assessed by the Commission services at the drafting stage of the proposal. Indeed, the IA guidelines clearly state that "once identified the problem and its causes, you [Commission official] still need to verify if the EU has the right to take action (principle of conferral) and if it is better placed than the Member States to tackle the problem (subsidiarity principle)".[77] Likewise, as the IA guidelines require the Commission to establish "which policy options and delivery mechanisms are most likely to achieve" the objectives pursued by the underlying initiative, the Court might take this previous evaluation into account when determining whether the final measure complies with the principle of proportionality.[78]

---

[77] IA 2009, p. 21.
[78] IA 2009, p. 28.

Proportionality is a general principle of European law, and may constitute a ground of challenge to EU action.[79] Lacking a precise definition within the Treaty, the meaning of proportionality has been largely defined by European Courts. According to established case law, a EU act is proportionate when is suitable (first limb) and necessary (second limb) to achieve its declared goal.[80] However, sometimes when the Court has found that the measure is both suited and necessary to achieve the desired end, the applicant may argue that the burden placed on him/her by the measure should nonetheless be regarded as disproportionate to the benefits secured.[81] However, it is clear from the case law that the Court undertakes this further (cost-benefit) scrutiny only when the applicants present arguments specifically addressed to it.[82] The onus is therefore on the applicant to raise arguments that place the matter before Courts and this is not, for obvious reason, an easy task to discharge. Yet, it is submitted that, given the increasing number of IA reports containing a quantification of both costs and benefits of proposed legislation (or looking into how costs are distributed within society), it will become easier for the plaintiff to gather this information and to use it in the proceedings. As a result, this trend might lead the Court to address more frequently the third limb of the test, such as to modify the nature of the proportionality scrutiny. Although

---

[79] Article 5.1 of the TFEU recognises the principle of conferral as well as those of proportionality and subsidiarity.

[80] Case 11/70, Internationale Handeslgesellschaft mbH v Einfhur- un Vorratsstelle für Getreide und Futtermittel [1970] ECR 1125.

[81] The existence of this third limb under which to check EU acts' compliance with the proportionality principles was clearly recognised in *Pfizer* where the Court stated that: "a cost/benefit analysis is a particular expression of the principle of proportionality"Pfizer Animal Health v. Council, n 88 above , para 410.

[82] P. Craig, EU Administrative Law, Oxford, p. 656.

EU Courts may decide that a given EU act withstands scrutiny under the suitability and necessity limbs of the test, they might still conclude, under this 'new' test, that the same measure is disproportionate on the basis of a cost-benefit analysis.

This example of spill-over effect stemming from the increased reliance on IA shows that the interactions between ex ante and ex post review might just occur without being neither deliberate nor foreseeable. Although transcending any process of 'juridification', IA may go as far as to shape those EU principles that dictate and constrain EU regulatory action.

4. IA AS AN 'AID TO THE COURT'?

Should the court be willing to consider an IA to determine whether a challenged EU act is in breach of the principles of subsidiarity, conferral or that of proportionality? One may wonder what kind of role these previous evaluations may play within such a final judicial determination. Could IA offer a useful aid to the Court in carrying out judicial review? What if the Commission has not performed these preliminary analyses? May the Court consider that in the absence of these preliminary assessments it is not possible to determine whether the challenged regulation conforms to the abovementioned principles? Would the Court be entitled/required to verify whether there exists a rational relationship between the final ruling on an act and previous examinations, such as an IA?

Some of these questions have been raised for the first time in *Spain v Council*, where the ECJ, after highlighting the lack of an IA by the EU legislature, found a breach of the general principle of proportionality and annulled the regulation contested by Spain.[83]

By an action under former Article 230 EC [today Article 263 TFEU], Spain challenged the new EU support system for cotton as enshrined in Council Regulation No 864/2003 by claiming that this new system, contrary to its declared purpose, was likely to encourage farmers to abandon cotton production in favour of competing crops, with serious consequences for cotton-dependent agricultural regions. In particular, Spain contended *inter alia* that fixing the amount of the specific aid for cotton at 35% of the total existing aid under the previous support scheme would not suffice to attain that objective, namely to ensure the profitability and hence the continuation of that crop. How and on what bases did the Commission services reach the conclusion that if set at 35% of the total existing aid in the previous support scheme that amount would suffice for attaining that objective? According to the Spanish government, the comparative study (cotton contrasted with other crops) of the foreseeable profitability of cotton growing, which was prepared by the Commission and used by the Council in order to determine the amount of the specific aid for cotton was incorrect, as its figures did not include labour costs. The inclusion of these costs would have entailed an increase in the production costs of cotton, such that adequate profitability of that crop under the new support scheme could not be ensured, so that that crop, contrary to the regulation's objective, would have been liable to have been abandoned.

Facing this claim, the court developed the following chain of reasoning. Building upon the opinion of Advocate General Sharpston,[84] the court recalled the scope for judicial review of

[83] Case C-310/04 Spain v. Council [2006] ECR I-7285. For a review of this judgment, X. Groussot, Judgment C- 310/04, (2007) Common Market Law Review, 761-785.

[84] Opinion delivered by Advocate-General Sharpston on 16 March 2006, in Case C-310/04 Spain v. Council, notably paras 82-96.

the principle of proportionality, in the context of the CAP. It therefore pointed out that, as the EU legislature enjoys considerable discretion in this field, the court's powers of review must be limited to verifying whether the challenged measure is not vitiated by any manifest error or misuse of powers, and that the authority concerned has not manifestly exceeded the limits of its powers. By referring to *Jippes*,[85] the court emphasised that "the lawfulness of a measure adopted in that sphere can be affected only if the measure is manifestly inappropriate in terms of the objective which the competent institution is seeking to pursue".[86] As a result, what must be ascertained is therefore not whether the measure adopted "was the only one or the best one possible but whether it was manifestly inappropriate".[87] Up to here the reasoning of the ECJ seems to be in line with its well-established case-law. But then the court adds:

> "However, even though such judicial review is of limited scope, it requires that the EU institutions which have adopted the act in question must be able to show before the Court that in adopting the act they actually exercised their discretion, which presupposes the taking into consideration of all the relevant factors and circumstances of the situation the act was intended to regulate". (para 122)
>
> "It follows that the institutions must at the very least be able to produce and set out clearly and unequivocally the basic facts which had to be taken into account as the basis of the contested measures of the act and on which the exercise of their discretion depended". (para 123)

---

[85] Case C-189/01, Jippes and Others [2001] ECR I-5689, para 89 and the case law cited.

[86] Spain v. Council, para 98.

[87] *Ibid*, para 99.

As has been observed, "this is new to the jurisprudence of the ECJ".[88] This seems to be true for at least two reasons. First of all, this assertion shows in an unprecedented way a clear shift towards greater judicial review of basic facts by the EU courts. Even if this trend was initiated by a line of well-known judgments, these have been judgments in the areas of merger control[89] and risk regulation,[90] and not in the area of the CAP. Given the high technicality of these fields, it is tempting to link the ECJ's greater scrutiny to a wider move towards evidence-based policy-making in the EU.

Second, although it would be unreasonable to interpret this judgment as imposing a general obligation on the EU legislature to perform an IA, the court is nonetheless pointing out that, when engaging in a (more intensive) judicial scrutiny of the basic facts which underlie an EU act, as triggered by a claim of a breach of the principle of proportionality, it might turn out to be useful have an IA at one's disposal. Indeed, what if an IA had been carried out by the Commission service in that case? According to the *a contrario* reasoning of the judgment, it seems that this would have enabled the court to assess whether the EU institutions "had exceeded the limits of what is appropriate and necessary in order to attain the legitimate objectives pursued by the legislation into question".[91] In other words, an IA would have

[88] Groussot, supra, p. 778.

[89] See, e.g., T-342/99, Airtours v. Commission, [2002] ECR II-2585, Case T-5/02 Tetra Laval v Commission [2002] ECR II-4381 and Case C-12/03 P, Commission v Tetra Laval [2005] ECR I-113. See Sibony and Barbier de la Serre, 'Charge de la preuve et théorie du contrôle en droit communautaire de la concurrence : pour un changement de perspective', (2007) 43 RTD Eur., 205

[90] See, e.g., T-13/99 Pfizer Animal Health v. Council, [2002] ECR II-3305. For an analysis of the standard of judicial review as applied to EU risk regulation acts, see A. Alemanno, Trade in Food – Regulatory and Judicial Approaches in the EC and the WTO, (Cameron May, 2007), 319-330.

[91] Spain v. Council, n 81 above, para 97 and the case law cited.

facilitated the court's task of determining whether the challenged measure "was manifestly appropriate".[92] What better way for the EU legislature to prove "the taking into consideration of all the relevant factors and circumstances of the situation the act was intended to regulate" than by producing an IA before the ECJ?

This reading of this judgment has recently been confirmed by the General Court in *Sungro SA et al.*[93] In this case, several Spanish companies claimed compensation for the losses allegedly suffered as a result of the adoption and application of the regulation annulled in *Spain v Council*. Although it dismissed the action (lack of causal link between losses suffered and the infringement of the principle of proportionality by the contested regulation),[94] the General Court took plain to explain that "it was not the contested provisions themselves, but the failure to take account of all the relevant factors and circumstances, in particular by carrying out a study of the reform's impact, before their adoption which was criticised from the point of view of an infringement of the principle of proportionality".[95]

A reference to IA was also recently made by the AG Maduro in *Vodaphone*.[96] Here though the IA report has been used to confirm the proportionality character of the Roaming Regulation and not to prove the contrary.

What remains to be seen, however, is the exact role that this analytical tool may be called upon to play within the process of

---

[92] *Ibid*, para 99.

[93] T-252/07, T-271/07 and T-272/07, Sungro, SA, Eurosemillas, SA, Surcotton, SA [2010] ECR, nyr.

[94] The applicants have not been able to establish that the losses that they suffered were connected with the infringement of the principle of proportionality which vitiated the contested regulation. They only managed to prove the link existing between their losses and the entry into force of the unlawful act by the Council. See, para 56.

[95] Para, 60.

[96] Opinion of AG Maduro delivered on October 1, 2009, case C-58/08 Vodafone Ltd, not yet reported, paragraph 39.

judicial review. Would such an "aid to the legislator" be susceptible to becoming an 'aid to the court' too?

As illustrated above, it seems that IA may provide already today 'analytical support' within the examination of the general principles of law, such as subsidiarity, conferral and proportionality. Indeed, to the extent that IAs contain a pre-legality check of the proposed legislation vis-à-vis those principles, it is likely that the Courts, when called upon to review the legality of adopted legislation, will refer to the IA analysis.

EU Courts may do so *sua sponte*, or under the pressure of the parties to the dispute. In any event, it is clear that the general availability and growing dissemination of IA reports will facilitate their encounters with ex post judicial review.

Yet, although it might be tempting for the Court to increasingly rely on these previous evaluations in order to support its judicial conclusions as to the lawfulness of the final act, IA as performed by the Commission services may not always be adequate to satisfy this task. This is because IA is currently carried out on the draft initiative put forward by the Commission and, despite the 2003 inter-institutional agreement on Better Lawmaking, is not always performed upon the amendments subsequently proposed by the Council and the Parliament later in the decision-making process.

VII. BEYOND 'JURIDIFICATION': THE CROSS-FERTILIZATION PATTERNS BETWEEN EX ANTE AND EX POST EVALUATION OF EU ACTS

After introducing the reader to the IA system, this paper made an attempt at examining the interactions existing between ex ante evaluation of Commission's proposals and ex post judicial review of adopted proposals. In particular, it speculated on which role IA analysis might play in the Courts' judicial scrutiny of the legality of European acts. It is clear by know that the possibility that pre-draft activities, performed under IA, might fall under judicial supervision, and more generally play some role at the ex post judicial review stage, deserves careful scrutiny.

For the time being, IA is not likely to be recognised as an 'essential procedural requirement' or as a substantive benchmark against which to assess the legality of an EU act. Therefore the Commission, like any other institution, is supposed neither to perform IA nor to stick to IA results during the regulatory de-cision-making process. However, this should not lead to dismiss as farfetched any possible interaction between ex ante evaluation and ex post control. Undeniably, given the growing number of IAs produced by the Commission every year, it wouldn't be real-istic to expect that their results would not have some impact on the EU legal order. There are indeed different *loci* and shapes in which such interaction may take place.

As shown by the example of the proportionality principle, there exist more subtle encounter patterns between IA and judi-cial review. A trend towards quantification of positive and nega-tive effects of legislative proposals may offer interested parties a solid background upon which to rely when questioning the pro-portionality character of an EU act. This may lead the Court to embrace *sensu stricto* proportionality so as to change the nature of this principle. Consequently, the resulting newly developed judi-cial principle, in this case proportionality, would in turn shape the way in which IA is performed by the Commission services. Indeed, under the IA Guidelines, legal obligations and principles do, quite logically, influence IA and the scope of the analysis.[97] As a result, there might be an interesting circular dynamic be-tween ex ante analysis of proposed legislation and ex post analysis of adopted regulation. A similar pattern may develop also with

---

[97] IA Guidelines, p. 12.

reference to the principles of subsidiarity and conferral. In particular, the IA's subsdiarity check, given the strengthened enforceability of the underlying principle,[98] is likely to increase the very-low rate of judicial review of the subsidiarity principle. This might in turn lead the Court to overturn and further develop its case law on Article 5 TEU, so as to trigger a reshaping of the principle of subsidiarity.

IA is not only developing as an 'aid to the parties' in dispute, but also as a potential 'aid to the Courts'. Indeed, as suggested by *Spain/Council* and the more recent Opinion in *Vodaphone*, an ex ante 'legality check' contained in an IA Report may provide 'analytical support' during the ex post scrutiny of the same general principles of law. There's indeed no reason why the Courts, called upon to review the legality of a EU act, would not glance at its IA Report and employ it as a useful benchmark. This is not to say that the Courts will necessarily find illegal those EU acts which have departed from the IA results, but that Courts may instinctively look at those results during their legality review. The IA Report, being part of the *travaux préparatoires*, may indeed disclose useful information on the pre-legality check and intentions of the legislator.

Our analysis shows that it is somehow inevitable that, given the high number of possible encounters between ex ante and ex post analysis, IA and its methodologies will find some room within judicial review. Yet this won't necessarily happen as a result of a 'juridification' of the IA process as such. Rather this is more likely to occur through a more subtle phenomenon of cross-fertilisation between ex ante scrutiny and ex post control methodologies.

---

[98] Article 5.3 TEU, Article 12 (b) and Article 8 of Protocol 2 on the application of the principles of subsidiarity and proportionality.

When this will occur? It is happening right now, but –as is often the case in the legal world– the results of these encounters won't be visible for a while.

BIBLIOGRAPHY

ALEMANNO, A. (2008), « *Quis Custodet Custodes* dans le cadre de l'initiative Mieux Légiférer? Une analyse des mécanismes de surveillance règlementaire au sein de la Commission et la création du Comité d'évaluation des études d'impact », *Revue du droit de l'Union européenne* 1, 43-86.

ALEMANNO, A. (2009), "The Better Regulation Initiative at the Judicial Gate – A Trojan Horse within the Commission's walls or the way forwards?", *15 European Law J.* (3), 382-401.

ALLIO L. (2007), "Better Regulation in the European Commission". In: Kirkpatrick C. and Parker D. (eds), *Regulatory Impact Assessment: Towards Better Regulation?*, Edward Elgar Publishing.

BRICKMAN, Jasanoff and Ilgen (1985), *Controlling Chemicals: The Politics of Regulation in Europe and the United States*, Itaha, New York, Cornell University Press, p. 305.

CECOT C., Hahn R., Renda A. (2007), *A Statistical Analysis of the Quality of Impact Assessment in the European Union*, AEI-Brookings Joint Center WP 07-09, May 2007

CROWE G. (2005), "Tools for the control of political and administrative agents: impact assessment and administrative governance in the European Union". In Hoffman H.C.H. and Turk A.H., *EU Administrative Governance*, Edward Elgar Publishing,

ELLIOTT E.D. (1994), "TQM[5]-ing OMB: or why regulatory review under executive order 12,291 works poorly an what president Clinton should do about", *57 L. & Contemp. Probs.* 167.

GELLHORN AND BYSE'S *ADMINISTRATIVE LAW, Cases and Comments*, Revised 10th Edition, by Strauss, Rakoff, and Farina (University Casebook Series)

GILARDI, F. (2002). "Policy Credibility and delegation to independent regulatory agencies: a comparative empirical analysis", *9:9 Journal of European Public Policy* 873.

GRAHAM J.D.(2007), *The Evolving Role of the U.S. Office of Management and Budget in Regulatory Policy*, AEI-Brookings Joint Centre for Regulatory Studies, Working Paper 07-04, February 2007.

GROUSSOT X. (2007), Judgment C-314/04, *Common Market Law Review*, pp. 761-785.

HAHN, R.W. and R.E. Litan (2005), "Counting Regulatory Benefits and Costs: Lessons for the U.S. and Europe", *Journal of International Economic Law*, Vol. 8, No. 2, 2005, pp. 473-508.

KONVITZ J. (2004), "The Institutional Context for Better Regulation", paper presented at the Conference on Simple is Better: Effective Regulation for a More Competitive Europe, Amsterdam, 2004, p. 8.

LEE N. AND KIRKPATRICK C. (2004), "A Pilot Study of the Quality of European Commission Extended Impact Assessments", IARC Working Paper Series No. 8, University of Manchester.

LEFEVRE S., 'Interpretative communications and the implementation of Community law at national level', *European Law Review*, 29 (2004), 808-822.

MATHER G. AND VIBERT F. (2006), *Evaluating Better Regulation: Building the System*, City Research Series, European Policy Forum, London 2006.

MEUWESE, A.C.M., *Impact Assessment in EU Lawmaking*, The Hague: Kluwer Law International, 2008.

MISTÒ M. (2003), « La collégialité de la Commission européenne », *Revue du Droit de l'Union européenne*, pp. 189 ss.

OBRADOVIC, Daniela & Alonso Vizcaino, José (2006). "Good Governance Requirements concerning the Participation of Interest Groups in EU Consultation", *43 Common Market Law Review* 1049-1085.

RADAELLI C. (2009), "The Political Consequences of Regulatory Impact Assessment", Paper delivered to the conference *Governing the Regulatory State? Comparing Strategies and Instruments*, British Academy, London, 15 January 2009.

RADAELLI C. (2004), "The Diffusion of Regulatory Impact Analysis in OECD Countries: Best Practices or Lesson-Drawing?", *European Journal of Political Research*, 43(5), pp. 723-747

RADAELLI, C. and De Francesco F. (2007), *Regulatory Quality in Europe: Concepts, Measures, and Policy Processes*, Manchester University Press, Manchester.

RENDA A. (2006), *Impact Assessment in the EU: The State of the Art and the Art of the State*, CEPS Paperbacks.

REVESZ & LIVERMORE, *Retaking Rationality – How Cost-Benefit Analysis Can Better Protect the Environment and our Health*, Oxford, 2009.

TIMMERMANS C.W.A., "How to Improve the Quality of Community Legislation: The Viewpoint of the European Commission", in Alfred E. Kellermann, Giuseppe Ciavarini Azzi, Rex Deighton-Smith, Scott H. Jacobs and T. Koopmans, *Improving the Quality of Legislation in Europe*, MNP, 1998.

VIBERT F. (2004), *The EU's New System of Regulatory Impact Assessment* – A Scorecard, European Policy Forum, London, 2004.

VOLKERY A. AND JACOB K. (2004), "The Environmental Dimension of Impact Assessment, Documentation of a Workshop organised together with the Federal Ministry for the Environment Nature Conservation and Nuclear Safety", 17-18 June 2004.

WIENER, J. B. (2006), "Better regulation in Europe", *Current Legal Problems*, vol.56.

WIENER J. & ALEMANNO A. (2010), "Comparing Regulatory Oversight Bodies across the Atlantic: US OMB/OIRA and the EU IAB", in Susan Rose-Ackerman and Peter L. Lindseth (eds), *Comparative Administrative Law*, Yale University Press.

THE PRINTING OF THIS BOOK,
THE SIXTH OF COLLECCTION
*CUADERNOS UNIVERSITARIOS DE
DERECHO ADMINISTRATIVO*, WAS
COMPLETED ON 30 OCTOBER
2   O   I   3

www.ingramcontent.com/pod-product-compliance
Lightning Source LLC
Chambersburg PA
CBHW071346210326
41597CB00015B/1558